Elementary Grade Three

Our TEXT BOOK Prophet Muhammad

Salla Allahu alaihi wa sallam

Life in Madinah

Dr. Abidullah Ghazi
Dr. Tasneema Ghazi

 IQRA' International Educational Foundation

Part of a Comprehensive, Integrated and Systematic Program of Islamic Studies

A Textbook for the Program of Sirah
Elementary Level Grade-3

Our Prophet: Textbook: part two

Chief Program Editors
Abidullah al-Ansari Ghazi
Ph.D. Harvard University
Tasneema Ghazi
Ph.D. University of Minnesota

Language Editors
Huseyin Abiba
Aisha Qidwae

Art Work
Saba Ghazi Ameen

Design
Saba Ghazi Ameen

Production Coordinator
Aliuddin Khaja

First printed in September, 2010
Second printed in April, 2013
Printed in Singapore

Library of Congress Control Number:
ISBN # 1-56316-150-8

IQRA's Note

This textbook has been designed to familiarize young readers the life and teachings of the Crown of Creation, Prophet Muhammad ﷺ in a straightforward and appealing manner. It conveys the contributions of Rasulullah ﷺ to the building of a flourishing world community based on faith, moral integrity and a sound social code.

Ideally, students will recognize the Prophet Muhammad ﷺ as the paradigm of devotion, piety and righteousness. We at IQRA' pray that the lessons offered here will only be the beginning of a lasting love for God's Messenger ﷺ imprinted onto the hearts of young students.

You will find this textbook written at the GRADE THREE READING LEVEL. In fact, we review the readability of all of our publications so that they match students' reading skills. We believe that this will be able to help them take hold of the concepts and values introduced in each lesson, thereby allowing them to adopt the Sunnah in their lives.

We at IQRA' suggest that teachers make use of the corresponding workbook to facilitate further reinforcement of the lessons. This workbook has been prepared to provide important drills in comprehension that will aid in the development of thinking skills.

In closing, we invite you to send us your comments and suggestions on this or any one of our publications. It is our ardent desire that the students using IQRA's comprehensive and systematic curriculum of Islamic Studies will be able to enjoy enriching themselves and their communities with a new and positive Islamic vision for life.

May Allah ﷻ bless us all on this voyage of learning!

Chief Editors
IQRA' International Educational Foundation

New Features

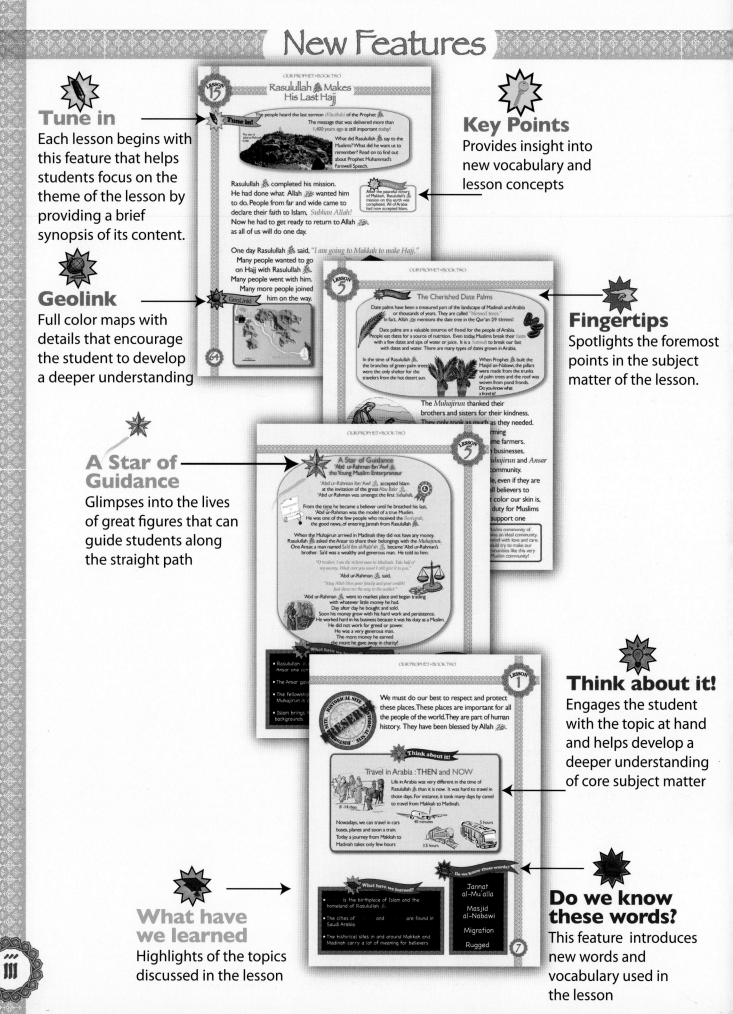

Tune in

Each lesson begins with this feature that helps students focus on the theme of the lesson by providing a brief synopsis of its content.

Geolink

Full color maps with details that encourage the student to develop a deeper understanding

A Star of Guidance

Glimpses into the lives of great figures that can guide students along the straight path

Key Points

Provides insight into new vocabulary and lesson concepts

Fingertips

Spotlights the foremost points in the subject matter of the lesson.

Think about it!

Engages the student with the topic at hand and helps develop a deeper understanding of core subject matter

What have we learned

Highlights of the topics discussed in the lesson

Do we know these words?

This feature introduces new words and vocabulary used in the lesson

The publication of this book was made possible
through a donation from the family of the late

Syed Moinuddeen

with the intention of Isal Ath-Thawab (إيصال الثواب) for him

Please remember him and all the believers in your Du'a

Table of Contents

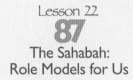

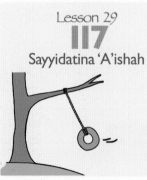

Two Special Cities: Makkah & Madinah

Tune in!

Every year, millions of Muslims visit Makkah and Madinah.
In the old days, the journey to Arabia may have taken months,
but today it takes about a day by plane.

Why are Makkah and Madinah important to us?
How far is Makkah from Madinah?
What are the holy sites located in these holy cities?

Allah ﷻ has blessed some places on earth.
We should show respect for these places and try to visit them.

For Muslims, the cities of Makkah and Madinah are very important.
They are places blessed by Allah ﷻ
and they are places blessed by Rasulullah ﷺ.

Makkah is the most important city of the Arabian Peninsula.
It is surrounded by rugged mountains,
as we can see in these photographs:

Prophet Ibrahim ﷺ and his son Isma'il ﷺ built the Ka'bah in a dry and hot valley called Makkah. During their time, Makkah was a completely empty valley. No one lived there. When he was there, Prophet Ibrahim ﷺ prayed that this place would be a safe and special place to worship only one God.

Our Beloved Rasulullah ﷺ was born in Makkah. He received the first *Wahi* of the Qur'an in Makkah. He first taught Islam to the people of Makkah. Even though he later migrated to Madinah, Rasulullah ﷺ could never forget his hometown. He loved it very much.

In Makkah, we find the House of Allah ﷻ, the Ka'bah. We can also find the house where Rasulullah ﷺ was born.

The graves of many important *Sahabah,* like that of Khadijah ﷺ, are in Makkah. They are buried in a place called Jannat al-Mu'alla.

Madinah, the city of the Prophet ﷺ, is a beautiful city surrounded by high mountains and date palm groves.

GeoLink!

The city is about 200 miles to the north of Makkah. This distance is about the same as:

the distance between New York City and Washington DC

or the distance between Los Angeles and Las Vegas.

We should visit this special place when we go to Makkah. This city is an important part of our history.

We can also visit the Cave of Hira where Rasulullah ﷺ received the first verses of the Qur'an.

When the Muslims of Makkah were tortured, many of them left for Madinah. Rasulullah ﷺ loved Madinah and its people very much. In fact, he decided to spend his last days in Madinah instead of in his hometown of Makkah.

Makkah

Yathrib

When Rasulullah ﷺ went to Madinah, the town was known by the name of Yathrib. However, after he settled down there, people began to call the city by a new name. They started to call it *Madinat un-Nabi,* which means "City of the Prophet", or simply Al-Madinah, "The City".

Al-Madinah al-Munawwarah

Over the centuries, some people started to call the city Al-Madinah al-Munawwarah, which means "The Brightened City." People call it this because of the Light of *Iman* that Rasulullah ﷺ brought to the city after his migration, the *Hijrah.*

There are many historical sites in and around the city of Madinah. There is the sacred Masjid un-Nabawi or "Mosque of the Prophet." Millions of Muslims visit this mosque every year. The Prophet Muhammad's blessed body is buried underneath the famous green dome.

We can also find the Battlefield of Uhud,

The Masjid al-Qiblatain,

and Jannat al-Baqi cemetery, where many blessed *Sahabah* are buried.

After making *Hajj,* most pilgrims travel to Madinah. They visit all these historical places to remember the life of Rasulullah ﷺ. Pilgrims visit his grave and the graves of the great *Sahabah* and offer their *Salam.*

We must do our best to respect and protect these places. These places are important for all the people of the world. They are part of human history. They have been blessed by Allah ﷻ.

Think about it!

Travel in Arabia : THEN and NOW

8 - 14 days

Life in Arabia was very different in the time of Rasulullah ﷺ than it is now. It was hard to travel in those days. For instance, it took many days by camel to travel from Makkah to Madinah.

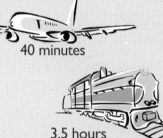
40 minutes

5 hours

Nowadays, we can travel in cars buses, planes and soon a train. Today a journey from Makkah to Madinah takes only few hours

3.5 hours

What have we learned?

- Arabia is the birthplace of Islam and the homeland of Rasulullah ﷺ.

- The cities of Makkah and Madinah are found in Saudi Arabia.

- The historical sites in and around Makkah and Madinah carry a lot of meaning for believers

Do we know these words?

Jannat al-Mu'alla

Masjid al-Nabawi

Migration

Rugged

The Kuffar try to kill Rasullullah ﷺ

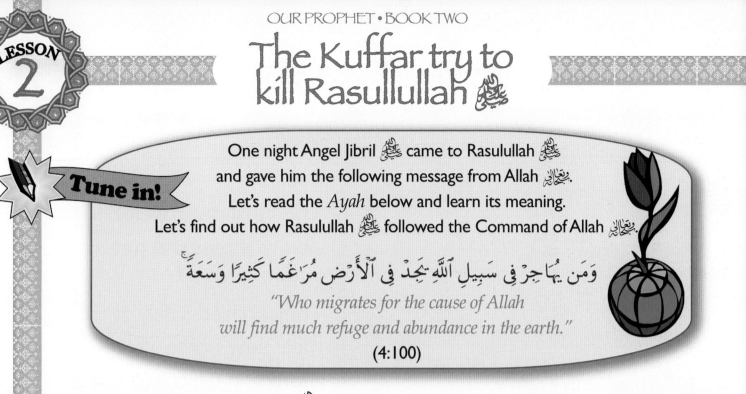

Tune in!

One night Angel Jibril ﷺ came to Rasulullah ﷺ and gave him the following message from Allah ﷻ.
Let's read the *Ayah* below and learn its meaning.
Let's find out how Rasulullah ﷺ followed the Command of Allah ﷻ.

وَمَن يُهَاجِرْ فِي سَبِيلِ ٱللَّهِ تَجِدْ فِي ٱلْأَرْضِ مُرَاغَمًا كَثِيرًا وَسَعَةً

*"Who migrates for the cause of Allah
will find much refuge and abundance in the earth."*

(4:100)

Prophet Muhammad ﷺ taught Islam to the people of Makkah for thirteen years. Yet many people still did not want to follow Allah's way. Many of them wanted to harm the Muslims. Some of them even made plans to kill Rasulullah ﷺ.

In the meantime, many people embraced Islam in a city called Yathrib. Yathrib was about 200 miles to the north of Makkah. Rasulullah ﷺ told the believers to go to Yathrib. They would be safe from the *Kuffar* there.

Since Yathrib was far from Makkah, it took many weeks to get there. The Muslims departed Makkah in small groups. They did not want the *Kuffar* to notice them leaving

GeoLink!

The Muslims traveled slowly across the hot empty desert. They arrived safely in their new home after a long and difficult journey.

The Muslims of Yathrib loved Rasulullah ﷺ very much. They also wanted to help the Believers from Makkah. They promised to keep them safe. They said,

"Welcome to Yathrib!
You are our brothers and sisters!
Come and live with us in peace!"

After most of the Muslims departed Makkah, Rasulullah ﷺ decided it was time for him to go too. The *Kuffar* were very angry when they found out that the believers had left for Yathrib. They were worried that Islam was spreading to other places.

They decided to kill Rasulullah ﷺ. If they did this, Islam would be finished. Then everyone would go back to their old ways.

One night several of Rasulullah's enemies went to his house. They had swords and spears in their hands. They were going to kill Rasulullah ﷺ and put an end to Islam. They said,

"We will wait here. We will kill him late at night when it is dark. Then no one will know who killed him."

Then, they waited outside the house of Rasulullah ﷺ.

However Allah had another plan. While the *Kuffar* waited outside, the Angel Jibril عليه السلام came to Rasulullah ﷺ. He told him about what the *Kuffar* were going to do. He told Rasulullah ﷺ to leave for Yathrib right away.

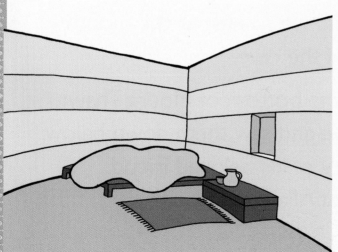

The Prophet's young cousin, Ali رضي الله عنه, was staying in the house at the time. He said that he would lie down in the Prophet's bed so the men standing outside his door would think that he was sleeping soundly in his bed.

Yathrib

Although Yathrib was to the north, Rasulullah ﷺ and Abu Bakr رضي الله عنه traveled south to Mount Thawr. The *Kuffar* would not think to look for them there.

Mount Thawr

When the *Kuffar* found out that Rasulullah ﷺ had left Makkah, they went after him. They followed the Prophet's path.

The Prophet ﷺ and Abu Bakr ﷜ found a cave high up in Mount Thawr. They hid inside of the cave so that no one could find them.

This is what the entrance to Cave Thawr looks like today.

Once they were in the cave, Allah ﷻ made a spider spin its web across the entrance of the cave. He then caused a dove to nest at the mouth of the cave.

Not long after, the *Kuffar* came to the bottom of Mount Thawr. Abu Bakr ﷜ peeked out of the cave and saw them down below. He became worried about the safety of his beloved friend. However, Rasulullah ﷺ told him that Allah ﷻ would certainly protect both of them.

Think about it!

Even though Rasulullah ﷺ taught Islam in Makkah for 13 years, most people there rejected his message.

Rasulullah ﷺ told the Muslims to go to Yathrib where they were welcomed and loved.

The *Kuffar* were angry that the Muslims left for Yathrib. They planned to kill Rasulullah ﷺ but Allah protected him and Abu Bakr ﷜.

LESSON 2

After some time, the *Kuffar* climbed up to the mountain with their swords and spears. They came to the edge of the cave. They were certain the two men were hiding in side. However, when they saw the spider web and the dove's nest they exclaimed,

"How can Muhammad be inside this cave? If he were inside the cave, the spider and the dove would not be here."

They gave up their search and returned to Makkah. Allah ﷻ saved our dear Prophet ﷺ and his companion with this miracle.

What have we learned?

- The Kuffar planned to murder Rasulullah ﷺ.

- The Angel Jibril ﷺ informed Rasulullah ﷺ that Allah ﷻ wanted him to leave for Yathrib right away.

- Rasulullah ﷺ followed the orders of Allah ﷻ and quietly left Makkah at night.

Do we know these words?

Embrace

Several

Mount Thawr

Exclaim

Think about it!

Allah saves Prophet Musa عليه السلام and the Children of Isra'il with a miracle

Musa عليه السلام was a prophet of Allah. He was sent to the Children of Isra'il.

His people were made slaves by the kings of Egypt. These kings were called the pharaohs. The pharaohs used to treat Musa's عليه السلام people very badly and made them do a lot of work for no money.

Allah سبحانه وتعالى sent Prophet Musa عليه السلام to save the Children of Isra'il. Allah told Musa عليه السلام to take his people from Egypt and move to a land called *Canaan.* Musa عليه السلام and his people planned their escape.

One night, they all left for this new home. However, after a few days they reached the shores of the *Red Sea,* where the pharaoh caught them with his army.

Musa عليه السلام asked for Allah's سبحانه وتعالى help. He threw his staff into the water. The sea split in two and made a road for the Children of Isra'il to walk on!

The arrogant pharaoh and his army tried to use the miraculous walkway.

But as soon as the last the person was safely on the other side, Allah سبحانه وتعالى commanded the sea to return to its original place. The pharaoh and all his men were drowned. In this way, Allah سبحانه وتعالى saved the believers by a miracle.

The Hijrah

A Beautiful Song

Tune in!

"The full moon rises over us from the valley of Wada;

You gave us the light of Your faith.

We thank You O Allah!"

Do you know that the children of Yathrib sang this song to welcome the Prophet ﷺ ?

Our beloved Rasulullah ﷺ and his faithful companion
Abu Bakr رضي الله عنه stayed in the cave on Mount Thawr for three days.
Then they left for *Yathrib,* which was about 200 miles away to the north.
They rode camels across the hot and empty desert.
It was a long way, but they were happy.

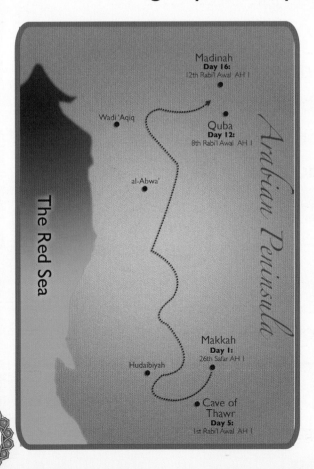

They were going to the new home
Allah ﷻ had chosen for them.
We called this event the *Hijrah.* It is
an Arabic word that means "migration."
This event is so important that the
Islamic calendars begins with it.

After two weeks of hard travel,
Rasulullah ﷺ and Abu Bakr رضي الله عنه
reached the city of Yathrib.
The people of the city were happy
to see them. Everyone came out
to welcome the Messenger of God.

HIJRAH OF OTHER PROPHETS OF ALLAH

We know from history that other prophets and special people left their homelands for the sake of Allah ﷻ. Here are a few of them:

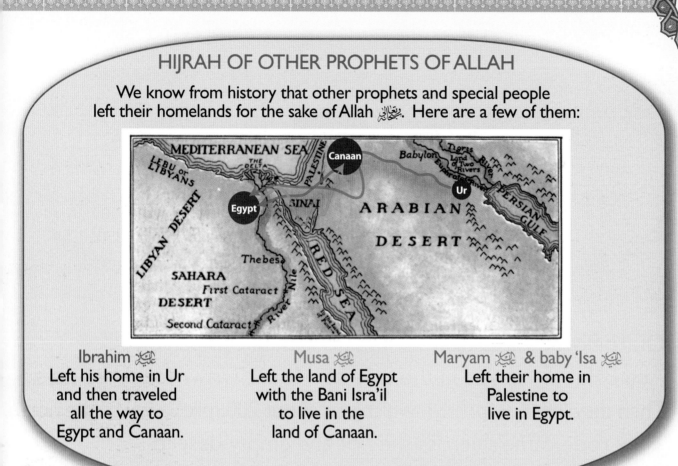

Ibrahim علیه السلام
Left his home in Ur and then traveled all the way to Egypt and Canaan.

Musa علیه السلام
Left the land of Egypt with the Bani Isra'il to live in the land of Canaan.

Maryam علیها السلام **& baby 'Isa** علیه السلام
Left their home in Palestine to live in Egypt.

All of the believers loved Rasulullah ﷺ.
Many of them wanted him to stay in their house.
Rasulullah ﷺ did not want to disappoint anyone so he came up with a creative solution.
He let his camel *Qaswa* loose and said that the house where his camel stopped would be where he would stay.

The people watched eagerly as the camel walked through the streets of Yathrib. At last, it stopped in front of Abu Ayyub's رضي الله عنه house. He and his wife were full of happiness to have Rasulullah ﷺ as their guest.

When the Muslims came to Madinah, they found the tribes of *'Aws* and *Khazraj* living there. These two tribes did not like each other. They often fought over the smallest of matters. We should know that Allah ﷾ does not like wars and fighting. He wants all of us to live in peace with each other and to take care of our planet.

Rasulullah ﷺ asked the *'Aws* and *Khazraj* tribes to stop fighting. After they became Muslim, he told them to accept each other as brothers and sisters. Since they loved Rasulullah ﷺ, the two tribes agreed to stop fighting. Islam brought them together in love.

The believers of Madinah took care of the *Muhajirun* (the Muslims who migrated from Makkah) and invited them into their homes. Because the people of Madinah were such a great help,

Rasulullah ﷺ called them *Ansars*, an Arabic word that means "Helpers". They were Ansars of:

Allah ﷾,
Rasulullah ﷺ,
the believers,
and the Message of Islam!

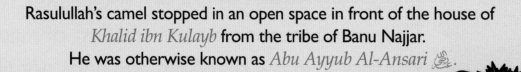

A Star of Guidance
Abu Ayyub Al-Ansari ﷺ

Rasulullah's camel stopped in an open space in front of the house of
Khalid ibn Kulayb from the tribe of Banu Najjar.
He was otherwise known as *Abu Ayyub Al-Ansari* ﷺ.

Abu Ayyub's ﷺ face shone and his heart filled with
happiness at being the one chosen to host Rasulullah ﷺ.
The Prophet ﷺ stayed at Abu Ayyub's ﷺ house
for almost seven months before moving to his own home.
Abu Ayyub ﷺ and Rasulullah ﷺ then became neighbors.
They continued to be friends and neighbors through out their lifetime.

Abu Ayyub ﷺ spent his whole life in the service of Islam.
Allah ﷻ granted him a long life.

What have we learned?

- The Muslims were not safe in Makkah.

- The Muslims in Madinah invited
  Rasulullah ﷺ to live in their city.

- The Hijrah is the migration of
  the Muslims from Makkah to Madinah.

- The Islamic calendar begins with the Hijrah

Do we know these words?

Hijrah

Qaswa

'Aws

Khazraj

Masjid ul-Quba & Masjid Un-Nabawi

LESSON 4

Tune in!

Look at the domes of the two mosques.
Can you tell which one is Masjid un-Nabawi?
What about the other one? Do you know its name?

Do you know which
was built first?
Let us find out in this lesson.

The Prophet Muhammad ﷺ has said,

"Whoever builds a Masjid on earth, Allah will build a house for him in Jannah." Sahih al-Bukhari

When Rasulullah ﷺ and Abu Bakr ؓ traveled together from Makkah to Madinah, they stopped at a little village called Quba.

Rasulullah ﷺ stayed in Quba for a few days. Quba is not too far from Madinah.

Rasulullah ﷺ met a few of his *Sahabah* in Quba. They built a small *masjid* and called it Masjid ul-Quba.

Fingertips

Masjid ul-Quba is the first masjid built by Rasulullah ﷺ and his *Sahabah*. Rasulullah ﷺ used to go to Masjid ul-Quba from Madinah and offer his *Salah* there.

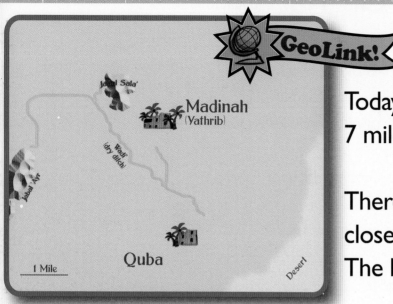

GeoLink!

Today, Masjid ul-Quba is about 7 miles from downtown Madinah.

There are many beautiful orchards close to the *masjid*.
The land is green and beautiful.

Masjid ul-Quba was the first *masjid* built by Rasulullah ﷺ.
He placed the foundation stone.
Later, his Sahabah finished building it.

It is great *barakah,* or blessing, to pray in Masjid ul-Quba.

"Whoever makes Wudu at home and then comes to Masjid ul-Quba and prays there, he gets the reward of making an 'Umrah." (An-Nasa'i & Ibn Majah)

The authorities rebuilt the ancient Masjid ul-Quba in 1986. It is a very big masjid now. It was a much smaller and simpler place before.

BEFORE

NOW

After Rasulullah ﷺ and the *Muhajirun* settled in Madinah, he decided to build a masjid there too. Rasulullah ﷺ bought a vacant piece of land in front of the house of Abu Ayyub Al-Ansari ﵃.

The blessed Prophet ﷺ and his noble *Sahabah* worked day and night building the masjid. They were very happy and thankful to Allah ﷻ for helping them build a place to pray in their new city.

The masjid was a very simple building.

The walls were made of mud bricks.

The leaves and the twigs of palm trees helped make the roof.

The trunks of palm trees became pillars to support the roof of the masjid.

The inside of the masjid was also very simple.

There was a large bench in one corner of the courtyard. People called it *as-Suffah*. Rasulullah ﷺ built this place for those believers who were very poor. The Muslims called the people who slept on the big bench the Ashab as-Suffah, or "Companions of the Bench."
Rasulullah ﷺ took special care of the Ashab as-Suffah because they had no families or homes. He spent a lot of time helping them.

Next to the *masjid*, the Muslims built rooms for the family of Rasulullah ﷺ.

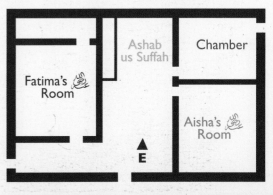

Ashab us Suffah

Chamber

Fatima's ﵃ Room

Aisha's ﵃ Room

E

Seven years later, the believers enlarged this place, now called the Masjid an-Nabawi. This was due to so many new Muslims coming to Madinah to meet Rasulullah ﷺ.

Rasulullah ﷺ and the Muslims were very happy and thankful to Allah ﷻ. They were grateful that they now had a *masjid* in Madinah. They began to offer their five daily prayers in the *masjid*. The Beloved Prophet ﷺ used to teach his *Sahabah* in the *masjid*. He received his many visitors there as well.

People made the Masjid An-Nabawi larger many times since the days of Rasulullah ﷺ. The most recent expansion took place in the 1980s. The size of the *masjid* is now very large so that thousands of people can pray there. The older section of the *masjid* where Rasulullah ﷺ used to pray is still there.

What have we learned?

- Arabia is the birthplace of Islam and the homeland of Rasulullah ﷺ.

- Rasulullah ﷺ helped build the Masjid al-Nabawi.

- The Masjid al-Nabawi became the first meeting place for the Muslims.

- Rasulullah ﷺ taught the Muslims in the masjid.

- The masjid became a shelter for the poor and needy.

Do we know these words?

Quba

Orchard

Ashab as-Suffah

Vacant

The *Ansar* of Madinah

Tune in!

The bond of faith ties Muslims together.
The Qur'an describes this bond in the following verse:

إِنَّ ٱلَّذِينَ ءَامَنُواْ وَهَاجَرُواْ وَجَـٰهَدُواْ بِأَمْوَٰلِهِمْ
وَأَنفُسِهِمْ فِى سَبِيلِ ٱللَّهِ وَٱلَّذِينَ ءَاوَواْ وَّنَصَرُوٓاْ
أُوْلَـٰٓئِكَ بَعْضُهُمْ أَوْلِيَآءُ بَعْضٍ

*"Indeed, those who believed and made Hijrah,
and struggled with their wealth and their lives in the way of Allah,
and those who gave them help, they are friends of each other."*
(al-Anfal 72)

Let's read about how Rasulullah ﷺ strengthened the friendship
between the Muslims of Makkah and Madinah.

The *Muhajirun* left Makkah.
They left their homes and their wealth.
Some even left their families.
They had almost nothing when
they reached Madinah.

Fingertips

The brotherhood between the *Ansar* and Muhajirun is called *Muwwakhat.*

However, the Muslims of Madinah did not hesitate to help the *Muhajirun*. Due to their unselfish support of the *Muhajirun*, we call these believers the *Ansar,* or the "Helpers."

Rasulullah ﷺ was sure that the *Ansar* would help their brothers and sisters from Makkah. They would help them settle in Madinah.

He invited all the believers to a big meeting. He said to the *Ansars*,

*"Our Muhajir brothers and sisters have left everything in Makkah.
They have given up all they owned for the sake of Allah.
I want you to help them."*

The *Ansar* were ready to follow their beloved Prophet ﷺ.
Each one of them adopted a *Muhajir* as his brother.
All of the Believers now lived like one big family.
This special bond of unity and love between the *Ansar*
and the *Muhajirun* is called *Muwwakhat*.

The *Ansar* wanted to share
all of their palm trees with
the *Muhajirun*. In those days
palm trees were a source of
money for the
people of Madinah.
They sold the dates and oil
that came from the trees.

The Prophet ﷺ knew that these trees were important to the *Ansar*.
He told them to share only the dates that came from the palm
trees and not the trees themselves. He did not want to make their
lives difficult. Allah ﷻ tells us that the *Ansar* thought more about
the *Muhajirun* than for themselves, even though many of them
were very poor. مِّمَّآ أُوتُواْ وَيُؤْثِرُونَ عَلَىٰٓ أَنفُسِهِمْ
وَلَوْ كَانَ بِهِمْ خَصَاصَةٌ وَمَن يُوقَ شُحَّ نَفْسِهِ

*"But they (the Ansar) give them (Muhajirun) preference over themselves,
even though poverty was their own lot."*
(Al-Hashr: 9)

LESSON 5

The Cherished Date Palms

Date palms have been a treasured part of the landscape of Madinah and Arabia or thousands of years. They are called "blessed trees." In fact, Allah ﷻ mentions the date tree in the Qur'an **29 times!**

Date palms are a valuable **source of food** for the people of Arabia. People eat dates for a source of nutrition. Even today, Muslims break their fasts with a few dates and sips of water or juice. It is a *Sunnah* to break our fast with dates and water. There are many types of dates grown in Arabia.

In the time of Rasulullah ﷺ, the branches of green palm trees were the only shelter for the travelers from the hot desert sun.

When Prophet ﷺ built the Masjid an-Nabawi, the pillars were made from the trunks of palm trees and the roof was woven from pond fronds. Do you know what a frond is?

The *Muhajirun* thanked their brothers and sisters for their kindness. They only took as much as they needed. Some of them learned farming from the *Ansar* and became farmers. Others started their own businesses. The love between the *Muhajirun* and *Ansar* created the first Muslim community.

Rasulullah ﷺ showed us that Islam unites people, even if they are very different from each other. Islam considers all believers to be brothers and sisters. It does not matter what color our skin is, or what language we speak. Allah ﷻ made it a duty for Muslims to establish friendship with one another and to support one another in doing right.

He ﷻ says: إِنَّمَا ٱلْمُؤْمِنُونَ إِخْوَةٌ

"The believers are all brothers."
(AI-Hujurat: 10)

> The Muslim community of Madinah was an ideal community. It was founded with love and care. We should try to make our own communities like this very first Muslim community!

A Star of Guidance
'Abd ur-Rahman Ibn 'Awf
the Young Muslim Enterpreneur

'Abd ur-Rahman ibn 'Awf accepted Islam
at the invitation of the great Abu Bakr.
'Abd ur-Rahman was amongst the first *Sahabah*.

Basharah = Good News

From the time he became a believer until he breathed his last,
'Abd ur-Rahman was the model of a true Muslim.
He was one of the few people who received the *Basharah*,
the good news, of entering Jannah from Rasulullah.

When the Muhajirun arrived in Madinah they did not have any money.
Rasulullah asked the Ansar to share their belongings with the *Muhajirun*.
One Ansar, a man named Sa'd ibn al-Rabi'ah became 'Abd ur-Rahman's
brother. Sa'd was a wealthy and generous man. He told to him:

*"O brother, I am the richest man in Madinah. Take half of
my money. What ever you want I will give it to you."*

'Abd ur-Rahman said,

*"May Allah bless your family and your wealth!
Just show me the way to the market."*

'Abd ur-Rahman went to market place and began trading
with whatever little money he had.
Day after day he bought and sold.
Soon his money grew with his hard work and persistence.
He worked hard in his business because it was his duty as a Muslim.
He did not work for greed or power.
He was a very generous man.
The more money he earned
the more he gave away in charity!

What have we learned?

- Rasulullah made the Muhajirun and the Ansar one community.

- The Ansar gave shelter and help to the Muhajirun.

- The fellowship of the Ansar and the Muhajirun is called Muwwakhat.

- Islam brings together people of different backgrounds.

Do we know these words?

Muwwakhat

Persistence

Generous

Basharah

Ideal

25

Building Unity and Harmony

Tune in!

Prophet Muhammad ﷺ showed us that good communities are built on respect and trust.
As the leader of Madinah, he treated the people with love, kindness and care.

FOOD BANK

As a great leader, Rasulullah ﷺ showed the world how to maintain a community based on love, peace and justice.

Rasulullah ﷺ established harmony among different groups of people in Madinah.

When Rasulullah ﷺ came to Madinah, there were many different groups already living there. People belonged to different tribes.

Rasulullah ﷺ wanted to bring harmony to everyone. Harmony means living together in peace with everybody. Allah ﷻ sent Prophet Muhammad ﷺ to bring people together. *Al-Hamdulillah,* we are Muslims and we believe in living in harmony with others.

LESSON
6

Rasulullah ﷺ made Muslims and non-Muslims feel safe in Madinah. He visited the leaders of all the different communities. He treated the people's leaders with respect and kindness. People loved him because of his generosity.

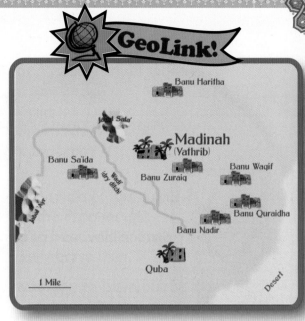

GeoLink!

Banu Haritha

Jabal Sala'

Madinah
(Yathrib)

Banu Sa'ida

Banu Waqif

Wadi
(dry ditch)

Banu Zuraiq

Banu Quraidha

Banu Nadir

Quba

1 Mile

Desert

There were several small villages around Madinah. Some of them were Muslim and some of them were Jewish.

Charter of Madinah

EVERYONE IN MADINAH IS FREE TO FOLLOW HIS OR HER OWN RELIGION.

EVERYONE WILL DEFEND MADINAH IF THE CITY IS ATTACKED.

ALL DISPUTES WILL BE JUDGED BY RASULULLAH ﷺ.

NO ONE WILL BE PUNISHED FOR LEAVING MADINAH.

Rasulullah ﷺ signed an agreement with the Jewish tribes living in Madinah. This agreement gave everyone the right to follow whatever religion he or she wanted. The agreement also said that everyone in Madinah should help each other.

We call this agreement the "Charter of Madinah".

The people of Madinah finally had a leader that everyone trusted. The Muslims especially obeyed Rasulullah ﷺ. They believed he was the Messenger of God.

27

Rasulullah ﷺ told both the Muslims and the Jews of Madinah to talk to each other about important matters. By discussing their problems together, they were able to choose the best solutions for all of them. We call this way of discussing matters *Shura* in Arabic.

Rasulullah ﷺ taught people to respect their neighbors, even if they belonged to different religions or tribes. Respecting people is an important part of building a peaceful community.

What have we learned?

- Rasulullah ﷺ brought harmony to Madinah.

- Prophet Muhammad ﷺ signed an agreement with the Jewish tribes of Madinah.

- We call this agreement the "Charter of Madinah".

- To live peacefully, people have to respect one another.

Do we know these words?

Solution

Generosity

Conflict

Mutual

Charter of Madinah

Think about it!

Harmony

Read the statements below. Do they show actions that will bring harmony or conflict? If they show harmony then put an **H** next to the statement. If they will bring conflict then put a **C,** and write how to turn the situation in one of harmony.

Show respect towards the members of other communities.

Show disrespect to the leaders of other communities.

Decide matters of community with *shura* (mutual consultation)

Participate in community service with our neighbors and other members of the community.

Make fun of people of other faiths.

Help the older people of every community.

The *Kuffar* Become Angry

LESSON 7

Tune in!

Remember how Allah ﷻ helped
Rasulullah ﷺ escape from Makkah?
He escaped and no one could see him...
He reached Madinah safely.

Can you imagine the anger of those who disliked Rasulullah ﷺ ?
Let's read this lesson and find out!

The *Kuffar* of Makkah were very angry.
Rasulullah ﷺ had escaped from them.
He was now the leader of Madinah.

Most of the people in Madinah were now Muslim.
They had become the *Sahabah* of Rasulullah ﷺ.
They were the *Ansar,*
the "Helpers" of Islam.
They were the *Muhajirun* as well.

The *Kuffar* were afraid.

"Now the Muslims
will become strong!"

they said to each other.
Their leaders got together.

"We have to do something.
We have to stop the spread of Islam.
Let us fight the Muslims!"

they shouted.

At that time, a handful people in Madinah said, *"We are Muslims,"* but they did not truly believe in Islam.

They were dishonest and only pretended to believe in Allah ﷻ and His Messenger. In their hearts, they did not like the Muslims.

Allah ﷻ called those people *Munafiqun.* A *Munafiq* was someone who said one thing, and did something else.

The Jewish tribes lived around the city of Madinah

There were also a few Jewish tribes living around Madinah. They followed Prophet Musa ﷺ. Allah sent Prophet Musa ﷺ with a book called the Tawrat. Muslims also believe that the Tawrat was sent by Allah ﷻ to Prophet Musa ﷺ.

Even though most of the Jewish people in Madinah did not believe that Rasulullah ﷺ was a prophet, they wanted to live in peace with the Muslims. Rasulullah ﷺ made an agreement with their leaders. This agreement was called the "Charter of Madinah," as we talked about in lesson six.

In the meantime, the *Kuffar* of Makkah began to look for people to help them fight the Muslims. Some of them said,

"The *Munafiqun* will help us."

Others said,

"Maybe the Jewish tribes will help us too."

The Makkan leaders said,

"We are rich. We have a lot of money."

We are more than the Muslims in numbers and our gods will help us win."

All of them said,

"Let's fight the Muslims! We will show them how strong we are!"

The *Kuffar* of Makkah got ready for war.
They were going to attack Madinah and defeat the Muslims.

What have we learned?

- Allah ﷻ protected Rasulullah ﷺ and helped him reach Madinah.

- The leaders of the Kuffar became very angry when they found that Rasulullah ﷺ had escaped safely.

- There were Jewish tribes living in Madinah.

- People who said they were Muslims but did not believe in Allah ﷻ and His Messenger are called Munafiqun.

Do we know these words?

Spread

Munafiqun

Munafiq

Defeat

Pretend

Badr: The First Battle

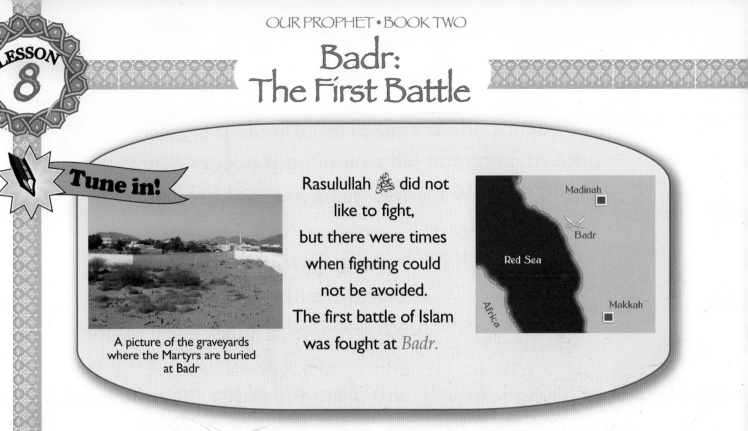

Tune in!

Rasulullah ﷺ did not like to fight, but there were times when fighting could not be avoided. The first battle of Islam was fought at *Badr*.

A picture of the graveyards where the Martyrs are buried at Badr

The Muslims made *Hijrah* to Madinah so they could be safe from the *Kuffar*. However, even after they moved, the *Kuffar* did not leave them alone. They did not want the Muslims to be successful in Madinah.

GeoLink!

The cities of Makkah and Madinah sit between the lands of Syria and Yemen. The people of Makkah were smart at business.

They used to travel to Syria in the north and Yemen in the south with their goods. They would go to the busy markets there and make lots of money.

They would travel in caravans. Caravans are groups of people traveling together with camels. To travel to Syria, caravans from Makkah had to pass near Madinah. The *Kuffar* were worried that the Muslims would attack their caravans.

The *Kuffar* of Makkah planned to fight the Muslims. They gathered more than a thousand men for war. They had many brave and strong warriors in their army.

Rasulullah ﷺ tried to avoid going to war with the *Kuffar*. When he realized that war could not be stopped, he asked Allah ﷻ for guidance. Allah ﷻ told the Muslims to get ready to defend their city.

The first battle between the Muslims and the *Kuffar* happened two years after the Hijrah. It took place during the month of Ramadan. The two armies met at a place called *Badr.*

This is a picture of Badr today. Badr is located about 70 miles southwest of Madinah. It is a very hot and dry place. Fortunately there was a spring at Badr that allowed thirsty people to have fresh water.

LESSON 8

There were only three hundred and thirteen Muslims. The Makkans had a much larger army. They had many fine swords and spears. They were sure that they would win. On the other hand, the Muslims were sure Allah ﷻ would help them.

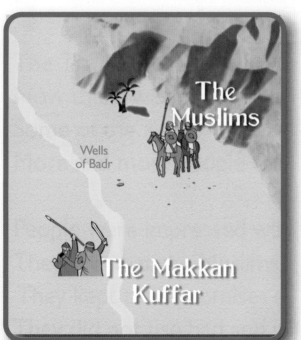

The Muslims

Wells of Badr

The Makkan Kuffar

When the fight started, the Muslims fought with great courage. Allah ﷻ sent angels to help the Muslims in their battle. Some of the *Kuffar* fell in battle and many more were taken prisoner. When the fight was over the Muslims had won a big victory.

The Prophet Muhammad ﷺ and the believers thanked Allah ﷻ for helping them in the battle. They knew that they won only with the help of Allah ﷻ.

The Muslims were kind to their prisoners. They did not bother them. In fact, they shared their food and water with them. Prophet Muhammad ﷺ said that any prisoner who taught ten Muslims to read would be free to go home. Rasulullah ﷺ treated knowledgeable people with great honor and respect.

Even those prisoners of war who could read and write were set free on the condition that they would teach Muslims how to read and write. It is our duty to learn to read and write as best as we can and keep on increasing our knowledge.
It is also important to share our knowledge with others.

Islam teaches us that reading and learning are very important.
The first word revealed in the Qur'an was "READ!"

Prophet Muhammad ﷺ has said,
"You should look for knowledge even if you have to go to China."
(Bukhari, Muslim)

GeoLink!

Rome

Persia

China

Pacific Ocean

Arabia

Makkah

India

Indian Ocean

What have we learned?

- The first battle between the Kuffar and the Muslims was at Badr.

- The Kuffar had more men and better weapons.

- The Muslims won the battle because they had faith in Allah's help.

- Allah sent angels to assist the Muslims.

- Rasulullah ﷺ treated the prisoners of war with justice and compassion.

Do we know these words?

Courage

Confident

Assist

Justice

Badr

LESSON 9

Obeying Rasulullah ﷺ

Tune in!

We Hear and We Obey!
Obeying Rasulullah ﷺ will give us
happiness in this world and the next.
The Battle of Uhud is good lesson on why
we need to obey Rasulullah ﷺ and what happens if we do not.

Let us find out what happened when some Muslims
disobeyed Rasulullah ﷺ at the Battle of Uhud!

We are Muslims and our religion is Islam, *al-Hamdulillah!*
Islam means "obedience to Allah."
We need to understand that obeying Allah ﷻ
means that we must also obey His messenger,
Muhammad al-Mustafa ﷺ.
Allah ﷻ says in the Qur'an:

يَـٰٓأَيُّهَا ٱلَّذِينَ ءَامَنُوٓاْ أَطِيعُواْ ٱللَّهَ وَأَطِيعُواْ ٱلرَّسُولَ وَأُوْلِى ٱلْأَمْرِ مِنكُمْ

*"O you who believe, obey Allah, the Messenger,
and those in authority among you…."*
(Surat an-Nisa': 59)

Key points

When we obey
Rasulullah ﷺ
we are obeying
Allah ﷻ

Obeying the Prophet ﷺ means
following what he taught.
We obey Prophet Muhammad ﷺ
because we love him.
We obey him because we know
he loves his *Ummah.*
We belong to his *Ummah.*

Allah ﷻ gave Rasulullah ﷺ
His last Book- the Qur'an.
Rasulullah ﷺ brought Allah's ﷻ message to us.
He showed us how to live the way Allah wants
us to live. In fact, his life was *"The Qur'an
in action,"* as his dear wife, A'ishah ﷻ, said.

When we follow the teachings of Rasulullah ﷺ, we will become
peaceful and successful in our lives. When we do not listen to
his advice, we make things difficult for ourselves.
This is what happened in the Battle of Uhud.
You see dear students, the *Kuffar* of Makkah were very upset
about the Battle of Badr. They did not like losing. They wanted revenge.

The leader of the *Kuffar* was
a man named Abu Sufian.
Just one year after the Battle
of Badr, he gathered an army
of three thousand men. Then
the *Kuffar* marched towards
Madinah.

The Battle of Uhud
was fought very
close to Madinah

When Rasulullah ﷺ found out about the plans of the *Kuffar,* he told
the Muslims to get ready to defend their city and their community.

After the Muslims gathered their warriors, Rasulullah ﷺ took them out to meet the *Kuffar* close to Mount Uhud. The Makkans had about three times as many men as the Muslims.

Part of the Battle field of Uhud as it looks today

Before the battle started, Rasulullah ﷺ ordered some men to guard a small hill. He put them there so the enemy could not sneak up from behind. He told these men not to leave the hill no matter what happened.

At the beginning of the battle, the Muslims fought bravely. They obeyed Rasulullah ﷺ and fought like lions. Soon, the Makkans began to lose courage when they could not beat the Muslims. Many of them dropped their weapons and started to run away. When the Muslims saw the enemy running away, they were happy.

A lot of them started to collect the weapons the Makkan soldiers dropped on the battlefield. They began to pick up all the supplies dropped by the *Kuffar* too. These things are called booty.

The Muslims guarding the hill saw what was happening. They wanted to go and pick up their share of the booty.

They forgot the orders of Rasulullah ﷺ to guard the hill no matter what. They quickly ran to collect the booty.

When some of the *Kuffar* saw that no one was protecting the hill, they stopped running away and got on their horses. They rode around the hill while the Muslims were not looking and started to attack the Muslims from behind!

When the other *Kuffar* saw this, they turned around to face the Muslims. They fought with great anger. This attack surprised the Muslims very much. They thought they had won the battle. Many of the Believers were killed as the *Kuffar* attacked. Many more were wounded. Even Rasulullah ﷺ was hurt. The Muslims began to panic.

When the Muslims found out that Rasulullah ﷺ was not hurt badly, they thanked Allah ﷻ. Their courage returned to them. They fought the *Kuffar* and pushed them back. When this happened, the fighting began to stop. Although the *Kuffar* did not win, the Muslims suffered great losses. Many believers became *Shahid,* or martyrs.

The graveyard of the *Shahid* at the Battle of Uhud

LESSON
9

There were many lessons to be learned from the Battle of Uhud.
Some Muslims failed to obey Rasulullah's ﷺ orders.
This caused the Muslims to lose many brave men.
They almost lost the battle as well.

Allah ﷻ told the Muslims to be patient.
The Battle of Uhud was a test for
them. He promised that they would
be successful only if they obeyed
the Prophet ﷺ.

What have we learned?

- The *Kuffar* decided to fight the Muslims once more.

- The second battle between the *Kuffar* and the Muslims took place at Uhud.

- Some Muslims disobeyed Rasulullah ﷺ and left an important hill unguarded.

- The *Kuffar* came from behind a hill to attack the Muslims.

- The Muslims suffered many losses because they disobeyed Rasulullah ﷺ.

Do we know these words?

Attack

Patient

Obey

Booty

Shahid

A Star of Guidance
Hamzah ibn 'Abdul Muttalib ﷺ

Rasulullah ﷺ once said:

*"Jibril told me that Hamzah is written'
among the people of the seven heavens…."*

(Ibn Hisham)

Hamzah ﷺ was the son of Abdul Muttalib, and an uncle of Rasulullah ﷺ.
However, he was almost the same age as the Prophet ﷺ.
Hamzah ﷺ was a very noble man. He liked to hunt wild animals
and be out in the desert. He was a very brave man.

In the beginning, Hamzah ﷺ did not pay attention to Islam but he did not
bother the Muslims either. He loved his nephew, Muhammad dearly.

One day Abu Jahl, a big enemy of Islam, passed by Rasulullah ﷺ and
began to insult him. He called him all sorts of horrible names.
Rasulullah ﷺ took all the abuse without saying a word to Abu Jahl.

Hamzah ﷺ soon came along, having just returned from hunting.
Upon seeing him at the Ka'bah, a woman ran out of her house
and told him every word Abu Jahl had said to Muhammad ﷺ. She told him,
*"If only you saw how Muhammad was treated by Abu Jahl!
with all the horrible insults, Muhammad did not say a word!"*
Hamzah ﷺ became very upset. He went to Abu Jahl and hit
him on the head with his bow. He shouted,
*"Are you going to insult my nephew now?
I am going to become Muslim! Hit me if you dare!"*
Abu Jahl was too afraid of Hamzah ﷺ to do anything.
Hamzah ﷺ went to Rasulullah ﷺ and said,
"You should be happy. I have taken revenge on Abu Jahl for you."

However, Rasulullah ﷺ said he did not want revenge.
He only wanted Hamzah ﷺ and the other Makkans to stop
worshipping idols and follow the Straight Path.

Later Hamzah ﷺ migrated to Madinah during the *Hijrah.*
He was a source of great strength for Rasulullah ﷺ and the Muslims.

Hamzah ﷺ fought fearlessly at the Battle of Badr.
At the Battle of Uhud, he gave up his life defending Islam.
He was buried on the battlefield. His grave is there today.
All the believers should visit his grave
and give him greetings of peace!

Asking For Advice

Tune in!

Rasulullah ﷺ sought advice from the *Sahabah*.
He asked their opinions about ways to defend Madinah.

Rasulullah ﷺ showed how Muslims should decide their affairs with *Shura.*
What came out of the talks was an effective way of defending Madinah.

What is *Shura?* How did Rasulullah ﷺ use *Shura* in the Battle of the Ditch?
Let us continue the journey of learning about the Prophet's life.

The Battle of Uhud did not stop the fighting between the *Kuffar* and the Muslims. Two years after the battle, the *Kuffar* of Makkah decided to attack the Muslims for a third time. They were not happy that they did not win at the Battle of Uhud.

This time they gathered a very big army. Men came from all over Arabia to join in. There were thousands of people ready to fight! The Prophet ﷺ made plans to defend the city. He discussed these plans with his *Sahabah.*

Rasulullah ﷺ listened to each one carefully. Finally, a *Sahabi* named Salman al-Farsi ﷺ made a suggestion that would stop the enemy from coming into the city. Salman ﷺ said that a deep ditch - *a khandaq,* should be dug around the city. It would be hard for them to cross the ditch. The Muslims would only have to fight those who were able to cross the ditch.

Everyone liked this idea. Rasulullah ﷺ said that Salman's plan was the best. He told everyone to get to work.

The Muslims dug a big ditch around Madinah. It was tough work because the land was rocky and hard. Rasulullah ﷺ and his *Sahabah* worked day and night to dig the ditch. With Allah's help the ditch was finished a few days before the army of the *Kuffar*. arrived.

Abu Sufian led the army of the *Kuffar*. When they reached Madinah, they were surprised to see the ditch. They did not know what to do. They could not get their army over it all at once. The *Kuffar* decided to camp on their side of the ditch.

Everyday a few of their brave men tried to cross the ditch. However, the Muslims were able to push them back. This went on for about a month. The Muslims kept the enemy from crossing the ditch. However, the *Kuffar* blocked anyone getting into or out of Madinah. The Muslims became worried because they were running out of food. Rasulullah ﷺ asked Allah ﷻ not to let the believers starve to death.

One night Allah ﷻ sent a powerful windstorm upon the *Kuffar*. The wind was so strong that it blew their tents away. Their supplies were blown away as well. Most of their animals became frightened and ran away into the night.

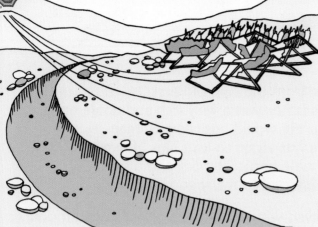

The *Kuffar* were scared. It was so dark that they could not see. Some of them thought the Muslims were attacking. They were also tired of sitting by the ditch for so long. They had enough!

By morning, they all ran away.

The Muslims were patient. They obeyed Rasulullah ﷺ. Now Allah ﷻ defeated their enemies. The Muslims thanked Allah ﷻ and said,

"Allah is One! He gave us victory!"

The Battle of the Ditch taught the Muslims many lessons.

First, it taught them the importance of making *Shura*. Islam encourages us to talk to each other about important decisions.

Secondly, it taught the Muslims to rely on Allah's help. Even though they were surrounded by a very large army, the Muslims never lost hope.

SHURA' (*Mutual Consultation*)

Shura' is an Arabic word. It means discussing with others before making a decision about some important matter. Muslims are required to make big decisions with *Shura'*. It should be applied to our families, schools and communities.

What have we learned?

- Rasulullah ﷺ consulted the Muslims when planning for the Battle of the Ditch.
- Salman al-Farsi ﷺ said to dig a ditch around Madinah.
- The Muslims defended themselves from behind a ditch.
- The army of the *Kuffar* of Makkah could not cross the ditch.
- After a month of siege, Allah ﷻ sent strong winds to scatter the enemy.

Do we know these words?

Ditch

consult

Shura

defend

righteous

A Star of Guidance
Salman Al-Farsi ⚜

The Prophet Muhammad ﷺ said,
"Salman is of my Ahl al-Bait, my family."

Salman ⚜ was a young man from the land of Persia.
Persia is now called Iran. His father was a very rich and noble man.
He loved his son very much. He would not allow Salman ⚜ to go
out of the house because he was afraid to lose him. However, Salman
decided to leave his comfortable home one day and travel.
He visited many places and listened to many good people.

Salman ⚜ visited a small town in Iraq. There he lived with a righteous old Christian monk.
Before he died, the monk told Salman ⚜,

*"The time has come for a prophet to appear in the land of the Arabs.
He will have the same message that was given to Ibraham.
After a time he will migrate from his city to another city,
one that has plenty of palm trees between areas of black lava rocks.
He will eat what is given to him, but he will not eat what is
given in charity. Between his shoulders there is the
'Seal of Prophethood.' If you can reach his land, try to do so.
For with him is protection and a clear path to God."*

Salman ⚜ began to find ways to travel to this land with palm trees and lava fields.
He found a group of Arab merchants who took him to Arabia However, they betrayed
him and sold him as a slave to a Jewish man. This man brought Salman ⚜ to Madinah.

Salman ⚜ heard there was a prophet in Madinah.
As soon as he got a chance, he went to Rasulullah ﷺ.
He gave the Prophet ﷺ a bag of dates as charity.
The Prophet ﷺ didn't eat them and gave them to the poor.
The next day Salman went again and offered the dates
to the Prophet. This time he said they were a gift.
The Prophet ﷺ ate those. He also looked for the
"Seal of Prophethood" between Rasulullah's shoulders.

When Salman ⚜ saw these signs he knew this
was the prophet the old monk had spoken of.
He immediately said his *Shahadah* and embraced Islam.

The Prophet ﷺ helped Salman ⚜ buy his freedom by planting
a garden of 300 palm trees in Madinah. The *Sahabah* donated the
saplings and helped Salman ⚜ dig the holes for the plants.
Then Prophet ﷺ himself planted the saplings in the ground.

As a free man, Salman ⚜ participated in the Battle of Khandaq, ditch.
When the Prophet ﷺ and the Sahabah were discussing the ways to
defend Madinah, Salman ⚜ suggested digging a deep trench around it.
This would prevent the enemy soldiers to cross the ditch and
enter the city. This plan worked and Muslims won the battle
without fighting. *Al-Hamdulilllah!*

A Community of Peace

Tune in!

When we meet our family members and friends,
we say *"As-Salamu Alaikum"* which means "Peace be with you".

Rasulullah ﷺ showed us the importance of building a community of peace.

Let us follow the story of Rasulullah ﷺ
and read how he established a community of peace.

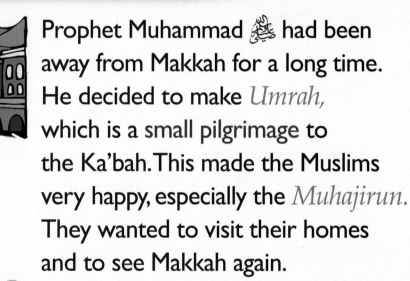

Prophet Muhammad ﷺ had been away from Makkah for a long time. He decided to make *Umrah,* which is a small pilgrimage to the Ka'bah. This made the Muslims very happy, especially the *Muhajirun.* They wanted to visit their homes and to see Makkah again.

The Muslims got ready to go with Rasulullah ﷺ.
They took camels, sheep and goats with them to sacrifice.
They started on the long journey to Makkah.

They did not take any weapons with them.
They were not going to fight.
It is *Haram* to fight or argue when you make *Hajj* or *Umrah.*

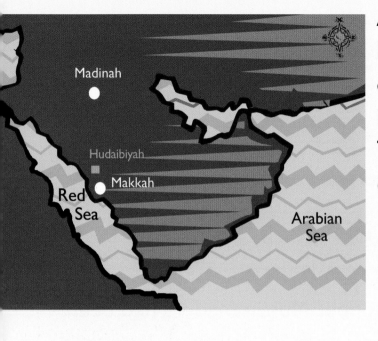

After many weeks, the Muslims reached the outskirts of the holy city. They camped in a little valley called Hudaibiyah. The next day they got ready to enter Makkah.

> It is *Haram* to fight or argue while you are in *Ihram* to perform *'Umrah or Hajj.*
>
> **Key points**

When the Muslims reached Makkah, the *Kuffar* did not let them enter. Rasulullah ﷺ and the believers waited outside the city. They did their best to get permission to make *Umrah.*

Rasulullah ﷺ did not want to fight any more. Some of the Muslims were very upset. They wanted to fight the *Kuffar* Rasulullah ﷺ reminded them that they came to make *Umrah.* He told them that they should not fight or even argue.

Rasulullah ﷺ decided to ask a great *Sahabi* named *'Uthman ibn 'Affan* ﷺ, to go to the leaders of the *Kuffar.* He asked 'Uthman ﷺ to tell the *Kuffar* that they wanted peace. Enough people had already been killed.

LESSON
11

'Uthman met with the leaders of the *Kuffar*.
They understood the Muslims did not come to fight.
They decided to make an agreement with the Muslims.

The *Kuffar* made a peace treaty with Rasulullah.
The treaty said that there would
be no more fighting between them
and the Muslims. It also said that
the Muslims could not make the
Umrah at this time. They would
have to wait for the next year
to make it. This treaty is called
the "Treaty of Hudaibiyah,"
after the little valley the Muslims
were camped in.

TREATY OF
HUDAIYBIYAH

• No more fighting

• Umrah next year

Many Muslims were upset when they heard
the *Kuffar* told them to come back next year.
They were not ready to accept such terms
of the treaty. Rasulullah knew better. He knew that any
agreement that brought peace would be good for everyone.

The Muslims finally accepted the
treaty because they trusted Rasulullah.
They packed their belongings
and returned to Madinah
without making *Umrah*.

50

Allah sent a *Wahi* to Prophet Muhammad ﷺ.
A *Wahi* is a revelation from Allah ﷻ.
Allah said that the *Treaty of Hudaibiyah* was a victory for Muslims.

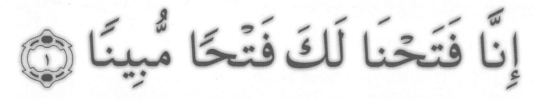

إِنَّا فَتَحْنَا لَكَ فَتْحًا مُّبِينًا ﴿١﴾

"Verily We have granted you a manifest victory"
(Surah Fath 48:1)

What have we learned?

- The Muslims wanted to make Umrah, but the *Kuffar* did not let them enter Makkah.

- Rasulullah ﷺ did not want a war. He agreed to sign the peace agreement with the *Kuffar*.

- This treaty is called the "Treaty of Hudaibiyah."

- Some Muslims were unhappy with the agreement, but Rasulullah ﷺ advised them to be patient.

- Allah sent *Wahi* saying the Treaty of Hudaibiyah was a victory for the Muslims.

Do we know these words?

Outskirts

Treaty

Agreement

Umrah

Wahi

Rasulullah ﷺ Writes to the Kings

Tune in!

Islam is a message for all people.
It teaches us that Allah ﷻ
is the Creator of everyone and everything.

Now that Islam had spread among the Arab people,
Rasulullah ﷺ saw that it was time to tell the people of the world about the Truth.

Let's see how he did that in this lesson.

The *Treaty of Hudaibiyah* brought peace to everyone.
Now there was no more fighting.
Some of the *Kuffar* began to listen to the message of Islam.
More and more people came to the Truth.

People were impressed with the behavior of the Muslims.
They saw that the Muslims were truthful, honest, and humble.
They kept their promises and respected others.
They did not use bad and rude language.
When they saw the noble behavior of the believers,
they wanted to become Muslim too!

Angel Jibril عليه السلام told the Prophet Muhammad ﷺ:

"Allah is the Master of everyone, Islam is Allah's religion. Islam is the religion for all people. Invite the whole world to Islam."

Fingertips

The Treaty of Hudaibiyah
was a great blessing
for the Muslims.
It brought peace so that
people from different places
could now learn about Islam.

Because there was now peace in Arabia,
people could travel without fear.
More and more people visited the Prophet ﷺ.
More and more people accepted Islam and followed Rasulullah ﷺ.
Rasulullah ﷺ told his *Sahabah* to invite everyone to Islam.
He told them to go and teach all the tribes about the Qur'an.

In those days, there were two powerful kingdoms near Arabia.
Rasulullah ﷺ decided to write letters to the rulers of these lands.
He was going to call these kings to Islam. If the rulers of these lands
became Muslim, Allah ﷻ would bless their lands.
The letters said:

Believe in One God

Believe in the prophets

Be fair to everyone

Do good deeds

Everyone will return to Allah

Everyone must fear the Qiyamah,
the Day of Judgment

Rasulullah ﷺ gave the letters to four of his Sahabah رضى الله عنهم.

He told one to go
to the ruler of
the Roman Empire.

He told one to go
to the ruler of
the Persian Empire.

He told another to go
the ruler of Egypt,

and the last one
to go to
the King of Ethiopia.

These rulers were powerful men.
They ruled over many millions of people.
Their lands stretched from the east to the west.
The rulers of the Roman Empire, Egypt and
Ethiopia followed the Christianity.
The ruler of Persia followed the ancient religion of Mazdaism.

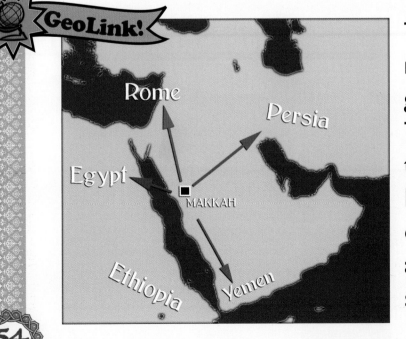

GeoLink!

The rulers received Rasulullah's messages. They did not want to give up their old religions. They thought that if they did, they would lose their power. In the *Hadiths*, it is said that only the King of Ethiopia accepted Islam, but he did so in secret.

Think about it!

People of the Book

Jews, Christians and Muslims are called the People of the Book. Read the following statements and write the numbers in the appropriate sections of the Venn diagram to the right.

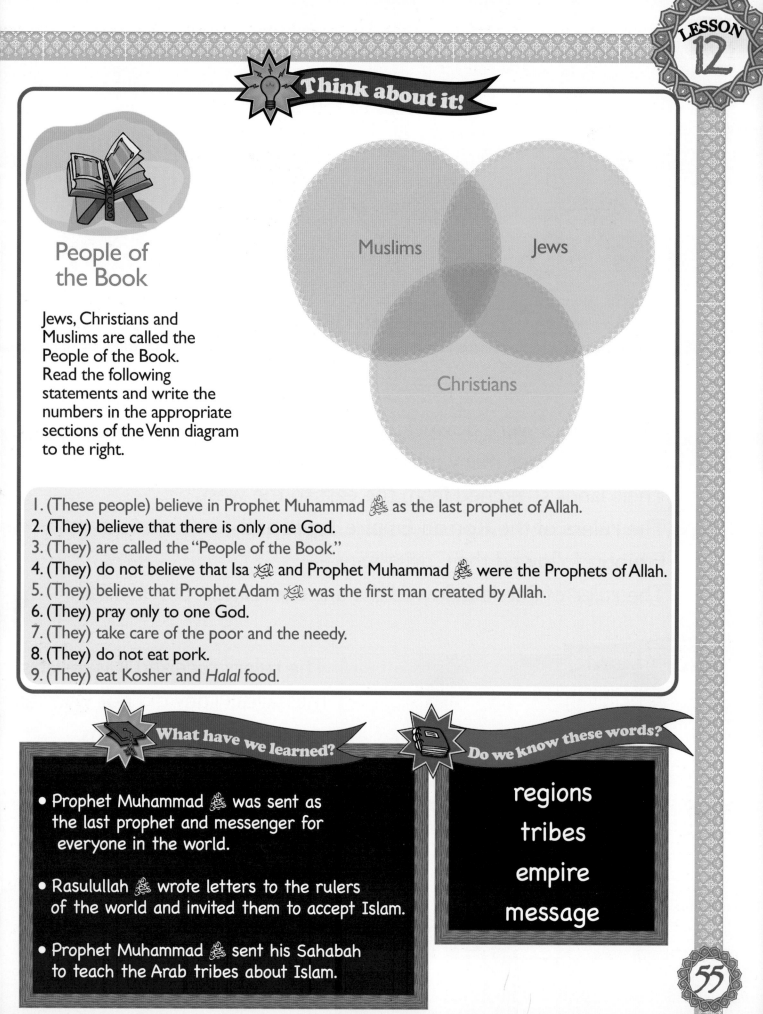

Muslims

Jews

Christians

1. (These people) believe in Prophet Muhammad ﷺ as the last prophet of Allah.
2. (They) believe that there is only one God.
3. (They) are called the "People of the Book."
4. (They) do not believe that Isa ﷺ and Prophet Muhammad ﷺ were the Prophets of Allah.
5. (They) believe that Prophet Adam ﷺ was the first man created by Allah.
6. (They) pray only to one God.
7. (They) take care of the poor and the needy.
8. (They) do not eat pork.
9. (They) eat Kosher and *Halal* food.

What have we learned?

- Prophet Muhammad ﷺ was sent as the last prophet and messenger for everyone in the world.

- Rasulullah ﷺ wrote letters to the rulers of the world and invited them to accept Islam.

- Prophet Muhammad ﷺ sent his Sahabah to teach the Arab tribes about Islam.

Do we know these words?

regions

tribes

empire

message

The Kaba Becomes Allah's House Again

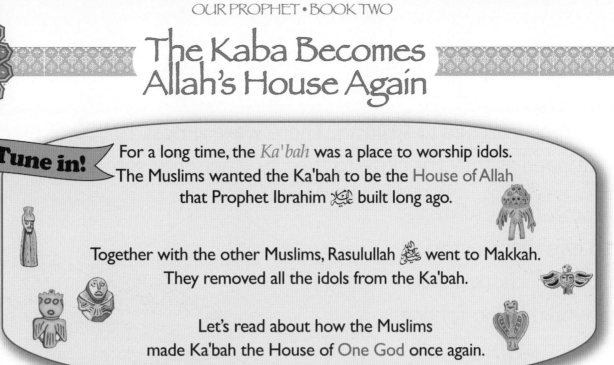

Tune in!

For a long time, the *Ka'bah* was a place to worship idols. The Muslims wanted the Ka'bah to be the House of Allah that Prophet Ibrahim ﷺ built long ago.

Together with the other Muslims, Rasulullah ﷺ went to Makkah. They removed all the idols from the Ka'bah.

Let's read about how the Muslims made Ka'bah the House of One God once again.

The *Kuffar* of Makkah were not happy to see Islam growing. They were afraid that they would lose all their power and wealth. Some of them wanted to fight the Muslims again.

One night, a group of *Kuffar* killed some Muslims. They broke the *Treaty of Hudaibiyah* by doing this. Rasulullah ﷺ decided it was time to bring peace to Arabia.

Rasulullah ﷺ called all the Muslims together. He said,

> *Allah has made us strong. We will go to Makkah and remove the idols from the Ka'bah. With our Lord's permission we will make the Ka'bah the House of Allah once again*

LESSON
13

The Muslims marched to Makkah. There were almost 10,000 of them! They stopped as they got close to the city. Then they set up camp.

They prayed that Allah ﷻ would give them victory. Rasulullah ﷺ hoped that there would be no fighting. He knew that the *Kuffar* would not be able to defeat such a big army.

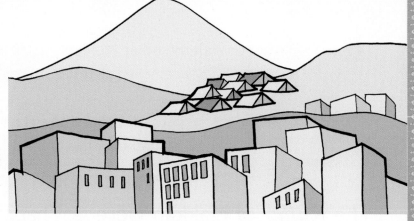

The leaders of the *Kuffar* understood they were outnumbered. They did not want to fight the Muslims.

Abu Sufian came out to meet with the Prophet ﷺ. He said that the Makkans would give up if Rasulullah ﷺ would not hurt them.

Rasulullah ﷺ was very happy. He agreed to Abu Sufian's request. He did not want to hurt anyone. Rasulullah ﷺ forgave Abu Sufian and all the others who hurt the Muslims.

When Abu Sufian heard Rasulullah ﷺ forgiving his enemies, he knew this man was a genuine prophet. He decided to accept Islam.

Abu Sufian went back to the people of Makkah. He told them,

"The Muslims do not want to fight. They want peace. We will not be hurt"

The Makkans now knew that Rasulullah ﷺ was kind and generous. They now knew that he was a prophet of peace. He truly was a messenger from the One God.

The Muslims entered Makkah without a fight. All of them went to the Ka'bah with Rasulullah ﷺ.

The Prophet ﷺ entered inside the Ka'bah with his beloved cousin, 'Ali ﷺ They took all the idols out of the Ka'bah. The Ka'bah became the House of Allah once again, *al-Hamdulillah!*

Everyone now saw that the gods and goddesses had no power. They realized that the power of the idols was in their imagination. They understood that Allah ﷻ alone has all power. Allah ﷻ alone is real and worthy. of praise.

The Muslims thanked Allah ﷻ for all His help. The *Kuffar* now knew that Prophet Muhammad ﷺ was caring and merciful. He was the prophet of peace and the true messenger of Allah ﷻ. They were no longer *Kuffar*. They were Muslims!

In the Footsteps of Rasulullah ﷺ

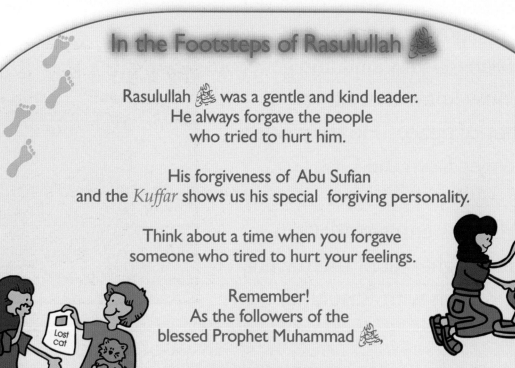

Rasulullah ﷺ was a gentle and kind leader.
He always forgave the people
who tried to hurt him.

His forgiveness of Abu Sufian
and the *Kuffar* shows us his special forgiving personality.

Think about a time when you forgave
someone who tired to hurt your feelings.

Remember!
As the followers of the
blessed Prophet Muhammad ﷺ,

we need to learn to forgive others,
even those who hurt us.

What have we learned?

- The *Kuffar* broke the Treaty of Hudaibiyah.

- The Muslims marched to Makkah.

- The *Kuffar* were powerless to fight the large army.

- Rasulullah ﷺ and 'Ali ؓ removed all the idols from the Ka'bah.

- Rasulullah ﷺ forgave all of his enemies.

Do we know these words?

outnumbered

generous

imagination

genuine

defeat

The Makkans Accept Islam

Tune in! The Makkans were touched by the mercy of Rasulullah ﷺ.
They accepted Islam. They said,

*"There is no god but Allah
and Muhammad is the Messenger of Allah."*

All the Makkans embraced Islam.
Truth and faith had finally entered their hearts.
Why did the Kuffar enter into Islam?
How did the Muslims help them understand the Truth?

We remember reading that Abu Sufian accepted Islam.

He was an important man in Makkah.

He spoke to the people of the city about Rasulullah ﷺ.

He wanted to make them feel safe.

The Makkans saw that the Muslims were kind and truthful.

They could see that the Muslims really believed in Islam.

When they saw this, their hearts softened.

They went to Rasulullah ﷺ and said,

"We have seen you. We have heard you.
now we know who you are.
Truly, you are a great man. .
You are Allah's last prophet. We accept Islam.
We say, La ilaha illa Allah, Muhamad Rasulullah

لَا إِلَهَ إِلَّا اللَّهُ، مُحَمَّدٌ رَسُولُ اللَّهِ

Please forgive us for what we have done.

Please ask Allah to forgive us. Please ask the Muslims to forgive us.

Rasulullah ﷺ smiled and forgave them. He said:

*"You are now Muslims. You are now our brothers.
You are now our family. You are now part of my Ummah.
I forgive you. Allah forgives you. The believers forgive you."*

There is great power in forgiveness.
Sometimes when we forgive those
who have wronged us,
wonderful things can happen.
The Makkans and the Muslims
were no longer enemies.
They were now brothers and sisters.

Fingertips

Prophet Muhammad ﷺ
showed us the power
of forgiveness.
When we forgive those
who have wronged us
it brings them
closer to us.

Rasulullah ﷺ not only opened the city of
Makkah to Islam but more importantly,
he won the hearts of his enemies.
They became believers and his faithful followers.

What have we learned?

- The Makkans realized that Islam was a religion of peace and justice.

- They were moved by the justice and forgiveness of Rasulullah ﷺ.

- They all accepted Islam.

Do we know these words?

Softened

Obedient

Realize

Forgiveness

LESSON 14

A Star of Guidance
The Forgiveness of Prophet Yusuf

A great example of forgiveness is the story of Prophet Yusuf and his eleven brothers.

HELP!

Their father was Prophet Ya'qub. Yusuf was a very obedient and handsome boy. His father loved him very much. Sadly, this made his brothers jealous. One day, the brothers planned to get rid of Yusuf. They took permission from their father to take Yusuf to the desert. Once they reached a deserted place, they beat young Yusuf and threw him down a well. To cover what they had done, they took Yusuf shirt and wet it with sheep's blood. They showed the shirt to their father and said,

"O father! Our brother Yusuf is dead. A wolf has eaten him."

Prophet Yaqub cried for his dear son. Nothing could make him happy.

A caravan with merchants came and passed by the well. They found the young boy, pulled him out and took him to Egypt. When they reached Egypt, they sold him to the governor of the city of Memphis. His name was 'Aziz. For many years, Yusuf worked as a slave. His honesty and faithfulness caused 'Aziz to treat him fairly. However, one day Yusuf was wrongly accused of a crime. The police took him to prison, even though he had done nothing wrong.

One night the king of Egypt had a dream. It was a dream that bothered him very much. He saw seven thin cows eating seven fat ones. He saw seven fresh ears of corn and seven dried ones. None of his wise men could explain what the dream meant. The king heard that Yusuf knew how to interpret dreams. He called Yusuf into his court and told him his dream. Yusuf explained,

"Your dream means there will be seven years with lots of food. However, after that seven years will be bad years with famine and hunger. You must save as much grain as you can from the good years so people can eat during the bad years!"

The King was very thankful. He realized that Yusuf was a wise man. He ordered Yusuf to be freed from the prison. He put Yusuf in charge of the storehouses where the food and crops would be stored for the drought. Many years later, the difficult time came. Hunger spread over the land.

It also affected the people in Yusuf's homeland. His brothers traveled to Egypt. They wanted to buy something to eat since Yusuf's plan gave Egypt a lot of food. The brothers came before Yusuf. They did not recognize him at first. They had not seen him for many years. They thought he was dead. Soon after, they realized who Yusuf was. They felt ashamed of their actions many years ago.

They begged their young brother to forgive them and Yusuf did.
The brothers were happy to have found Yusuf.
They brought their father to meet him. It was a beautiful reunion!
Afterwards, Yusuf family stayed in Egypt.
They were happy for many years.

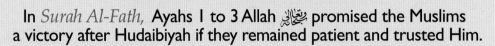

Think about it!

In *Surah Al-Fath,* Ayahs 1 to 3 Allah ﷻ promised the Muslims a victory after Hudaibiyah if they remained patient and trusted Him.

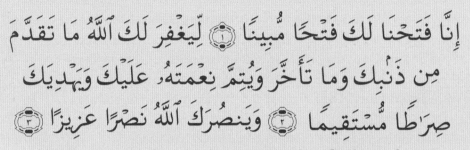

We have granted you a clear victory that God may forgive you your past and future shortcomings, grant you His blessings, and guide you to the straight path."

[Surah al-Fath, 48:1-3]

Read the above words of Allah ﷻ and complete the following chart:

Allah ﷻ promised Muslims that He would...	If they would...
"Give them a clear ."	
"Forgive their ."	
"Forgive their future ."	
"Grant them His ."	
"Guide them to the ."	

Discuss with your friends the different ways you can receive blessings of Allah ﷻ and then write these ways in your journal.

Rasulullah ﷺ Makes His Last Hajj

LESSON 15

Tune in!

The people heard the last sermon *(Khutbah)* of the Prophet ﷺ. The message that was delivered more than 1,400 years ago is still important today!

What did Rasulullah ﷺ say to the Muslims? What did he want us to remember? Read on to find out about Prophet Muhammad's Farewell Speech.

The site of Jabal ar-Rahmah today

Rasulullah ﷺ completed his mission. He had done what Allah ﷻ wanted him to do. People from far and wide came to declare their faith to Islam, *Subhan Allah!* Now he had to get ready to return to Allah ﷻ, as all of us will do one day.

Keypoints

After the peaceful victory of Makkah, Rasulullah's ﷺ mission on this earth was completed. All of Arabia had now accepted Islam.

One day Rasulullah ﷺ said, *"I am going to Makkah to make Hajj."* Many people wanted to go on Hajj with Rasulullah ﷺ. Many people went with him. Many more people joined him on the way.

GeoLink!

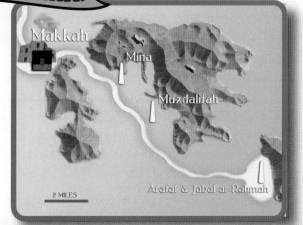

Makkah
Mina
Muzdalifah
Arafat & Jabal ar-Rahmah
2 MILES

Soon there was a big crowd. There were thousands and thousands of people. All of them were Muslims. They were all the *Sahabah* of Rasulullah ﷺ.

LESSON
15

"Takbir, Allah Hu Akbar!
Labaik Allahuma Labaik!"

The following day, after Rasulullah ﷺ had done his Fajr prayer, all the people left for the Valley of 'Arafat. They recited the *Takbir and Talbiyah* as they made their way to 'Arafat.

In 'Arafat, Rasulullah ﷺ stood on a hill called Jabal ar-Rahmah. He looked at all the people. All of them were his *Sahabah*. He thanked Allah for His kindness and help. Then he spoke to the people. It was his last speech to such a large group. He said,

"The bad ways of the past are gone.
Allah has chosen Islam for us.

Remember!
All human beings are brothers and sisters.

We are all children of Adam.
Be kind to everyone.
Do not kill anyone.

Allah alone is worthy of worship.
Fear Allah and obey Him.
Listen to what I say,
for I may not be with you for much longer."

The people listened carefully as he gave his last speech. It is called the "Farewell Speech" or the *Khutbat ul-Wada'*, because it was Rasulullah's last *Khutbah*.

LESSON 15

During the *Khutbat ul-Wada'*, the Prophet ﷺ reminded the Muslims of their duty to:

The Prophet ﷺ said

Be kind to women and respect everyone

Obey your leaders as long as they obey Allah

The best people are those who are righteous

Keep your promises

The Believers are brothers and sisters to one another.

Be responsible for your actions.

At the end of his speech, he said to the people,

I am leaving with you the Book of Allah, and my Sunnah.
If you follow them you will never be lost."

Then he asked the people:

"O people, have I given you Allah's message?"

They all answered:

O Rasulullah!
O Prophet of Allah, O Messenger of peace, You have taught us Islam. You have taught us the Qur'an.
You have taught us to do what is right. Truly you have given us Allah's message.

Then Rasulullah ﷺ told the people:

I have taught you what Allah has given me. I have given you the message of Islam.
Now, you teach this message to others.
Tell everyone what Islam is about.

The people replied:

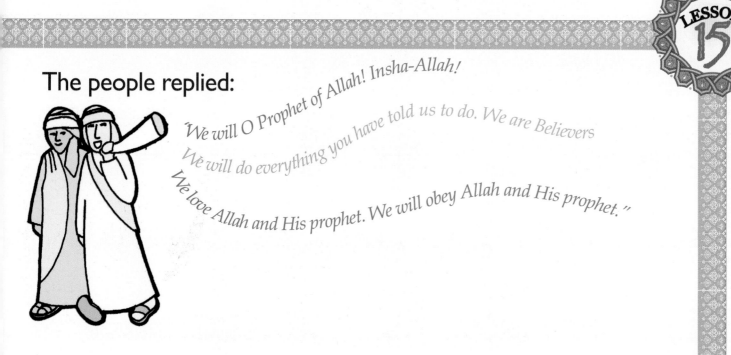

"We will O Prophet of Allah! Insha-Allah!
We will do everything you have told us to do. We are Believers
We love Allah and His prophet. We will obey Allah and His prophet."

Rasulullah ﷺ was happy that he gave the message of Allah ﷻ to his people. He told them to tell those who were not present about what he said. The Prophet ﷺ then left the Valley of 'Arafat to complete his Hajj.

When the people listened to the *Khutbat ul-Wada'*, they realized that Rasulullah ﷺ had completed his mission. They also knew that his life was ending. This made them very sad. They loved the Prophet ﷺ and they did not want to lose him.

What have we learned?

- Rasulullah ﷺ made his last Hajj together with thousands of Muslims.

- Rasulullah ﷺ delivered his Farewell Speech on the Jabal ar-Rahmah.

- The Farewell Speech was a message of equality, unity and justice.

Do we know these words?

Equality

Justice

Heeded

Righteous

Farewell

LESSON 16

Rasulullah ﷺ Leaves This Life

Tune in!

Rasulullah has passed away,
But from me he will never part.
For everyday I think of him,
From the bottom of my heart.

The last days of the Prophet ﷺ had arrived.
The people were sad when he passed away.
The personality of our dear Prophet ﷺ lives on in our hearts.
Find out how the Muslims felt when they realized that
Prophet Muhammad ﷺ would be leaving them.

After making the *Hajj*, Rasulullah ﷺ went back to Madinah. He spent most of his time in prayer. He soon became very sick. Every day his illness became worse. He could not even go to the *Masjid* to make his *Salat*.

Rasulullah ﷺ asked his best friend Abu Bakr ﷺ to lead the *Salat*. The people were sad since they could no longer pray behind Rasulullah ﷺ.

One day Rasulullah ﷺ felt a little better. He went to the *masjid*. The believers were glad to see him. He spoke and said:

"O my Ummah!
Learn the Qur'an.
Be regular in making your Salat.
Do what I have taught you.
Love and help each other.
If you do, Allah will help you."

Rasulullah ﷺ became very weak and he stayed in bed. The Muslims were very sad. They prayed for his health. They knew that only Allah ﷻ has power over health and sickness and over life and death.

Rasulullah ﷺ told his wife 'A'ishah ﷢
*"Give everything I have to the poor.
I shall leave only the teachings of Islam."*

He told his daughter Fatimah ﷢
*"Do good deeds my daughter. Help those who
are unfortunate. Certainly Allah loves those who do good."*

Finally, the time for Rasulullah ﷺ to leave this earth had come.
He became weaker and weaker. He said:

"Allah is truly the best of friends. Allah is the only True Friend."

Then our dear Prophet Muhammad passed away. He was 63 years-old.
Rasulullah ﷺ did the job Allah ﷻ wanted him to do.
He taught Islam to the whole world.
He showed people how to live as believers.
He was an example of a perfect human being.
Allah ﷻ tells in the Qur'an:

إِنَّا لِلَّهِ وَإِنَّا إِلَيْهِ رَاجِعُونَ

"To Allah we belong, and to Him is our return."
(Al-Baqara 2:156)

What have we learned?

- Rasulullah ﷺ had a fever and became too weak to lead the Salat.

- Prophet Muhammad ﷺ passed away at the age of 63.

- Believers are encouraged to do good deeds and to give money, clothes and time to help the unfortunate.

Do we know these words?

Believers

Encouraged

Deed

Unfortunate

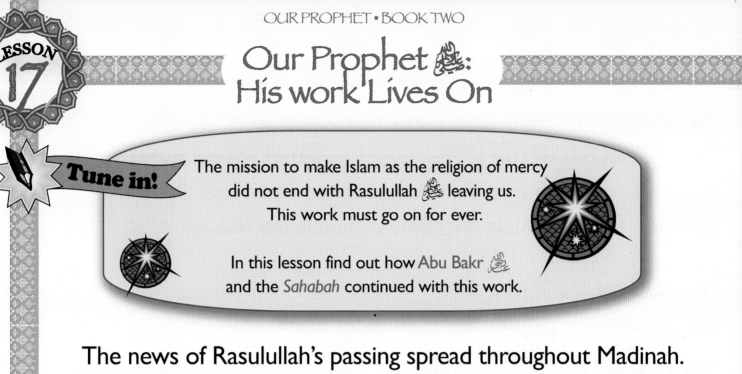

LESSON 17

Our Prophet ﷺ: His work Lives On

Tune in!

The mission to make Islam as the religion of mercy did not end with Rasulullah ﷺ leaving us. This work must go on for ever.

In this lesson find out how Abu Bakr ؓ and the *Sahabah* continued with this work.

The news of Rasulullah's passing spread throughout Madinah. Many of the *Sahabah* could not believe that he was gone.

Abu Bakr ؓ rushed to the Prophet's home.
There he gently uncovered the face of his dear friend.
Holding back his tears, he wished him farewell. He said,

*"You were beautiful when you were alive
and you are beautiful even now in death."*

Then he left the house to speak to the community.
Everyone was crying. Rasulullah ﷺ was no longer with them.
Abu Bakr ؓ knew people were sad.
He said many words that comforted them.

Rasulullah ﷺ taught that everyone has to pass away one day.
The Qur'an tells us that all the bygone prophets passed away too.
The *Sahabah* knew that Allah's last prophet would also die
one day. They knew that they would die one day too.

The *Sahabah* loved Rasulullah ﷺ more than their parents,
more than their children and even more than themselves.
They were true believers. They said:

" *Prophet Muhammad ﷺ is our master.
We love him more than anything.*

He taught
us Islam.

He taught us
to do good deeds.

He taught us
the Qur'an.

He did what
Allah told him.

*Now he has gone back
to the One who made him.*

*We will do what Rasulullah ﷺ wanted us to do.
We will teach Islam to others.
We will teach the Qur'an to all people.* "

LESSON
17

After Rasulullah's death, the Muslims chose
Abu Bakr رضي الله عنه to be their leader.
He became the first *Khalifah,* or successor, of Rasulullah ﷺ.
The Muslims were united under the new leader.

After Abu Bakr رضي الله عنه became the *Khalifah* he made a speech:

66 *I will obey Allah.*
I will follow Rasulullah ﷺ.
I will listen to the advice
of the Ummah in my work.
I will work for Islam with the help of Allah.
Please make Du'a that I will be a good leader. 99

The Muslims promised to obey their *Khalifah* and help him.

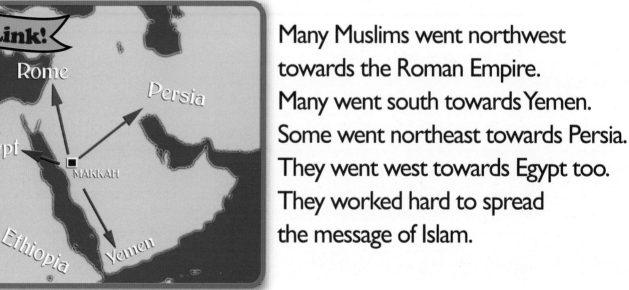

GeoLink!

Rome
Persia
Egypt
MAKKAH
Ethiopia
Yemen

Many Muslims went northwest
towards the Roman Empire.
Many went south towards Yemen.
Some went northeast towards Persia.
They went west towards Egypt too.
They worked hard to spread
the message of Islam.

The work of teaching Islam is not over.
Today, Islam and Muslims are often misunderstood.
Some people do not realize that Islam is a peaceful and merciful religion.

Do you know anything we can do to help people understand Islam?
A good start would be to study the life of Prophet Muhammad ﷺ.
We can learn how he explained Islam to his friends and neighbors.
We can follow his noble example and share Islam, *inshallah!*

What have we learned?

- The Muslims were upset when they heard the news of Rasulullah's death.

- Abu Bakr became the leader of the Muslim community.

- All Muslims have the responsibility to share Islam with others.

Do we know these words?

Spread

Realize

Khalifah

Misunderstood

Personality

Successor

The *Sunnah* of Rasulullah ﷺ: The Best Model

Tune in!

All Muslims love Rasulullah ﷺ.
We like to find out as much as we can about how he lived.

Fortunately, we know the *Sunnah* of Rasulullah ﷺ.
This helps us learn how to live our lives in a good way.

What is the *Sunnah?* Why is it important to us?

Let us read more about the life of Rasulullah ﷺ
and find out why learning Sunnah is important!

When Allah ﷻ sent His *Qur'an* to
Rasulullah ﷺ He promised to protect it.
The words of the Qur'an have never been changed.
The Qur'an is a book that has helped people
become better human beings.
The Prophet Muhammad ﷺ was
the example of a perfect human being.
The *Sunnah* is the example given by his life.

Taking care of and loving cats
is a *sunnah*. Rasulullah's ﷺ
favorite cat was named Muezza.

The *Sunnah* shows us how to follow
Allah's commands in our own lives.
The *Sunnah* includes the teachings of
Rasulullah ﷺ that are taken from his
words and actions.

From the days of Rasulullah ﷺ good Muslims tried their
best to follow the *Sunnah*. We can find the *Sunnah* of
Rasulullah ﷺ in books of *Sirah and Hadith.*

Hadiths are the sayings and actions of Rasulullah ﷺ written down. There are many books where we can find Hadiths.

What does the Qur'an say about the *Sunnah?*
It says that following the *Sunnah* is
important if we want to obey Allah ﷻ:

قُلْ إِن كُنتُمْ تُحِبُّونَ ٱللَّهَ فَٱتَّبِعُونِى يُحْبِبْكُمُ ٱللَّهُ وَيَغْفِرْ لَكُمْ ذُنُوبَكُمْ ...

"If ye do love Allah, Follow me: Allah will love you and forgive you your sins ..."
(Al Imran 3:31)

We must follow Rasulullah ﷺ if we want
the blessings and love of Allah ﷻ.
Rasulullah's conduct and personality
are the best models to follow. Allah ﷻ says in the Qur'an:

لَّقَدْ كَانَ لَكُمْ فِى رَسُولِ ٱللَّهِ أُسْوَةٌ حَسَنَةٌ ...

"Certainly in the Messenger of Allah you have an excellent example."
(Al-Ahzab: 21)

What have we learned?

- The *Sunnah* contains information about the teachings of Rasulullah ﷺ.

- The *Sunnah* is the second most important source for guidance.

- The *Hadith* are the sayings and actions of Rasulullah ﷺ written down.

- We read the *Hadith* so we can know how to practice Islam correctly.

Do we know these words?

Speech

Experience

Deviated

Sunnah

Hadith

LESSON 19

A Day with Rasulullah ﷺ

Tune in!

Every single day of Prophet Muhammad's life was filled with activity from morning until night. Still, he never missed any of his prayers.

In fact, he prayed more than anyone else.

How did Rasulullah ﷺ spend his day? What did he do in the morning, afternoon, evening and night?

Rasulullah ﷺ had a very busy schedule every day. He spent his time praying, teaching, helping people with problems, and looking after both his family and the community.

FAJR TIME

Early in the morning when Rasulullah ﷺ heard the *Adhan,* he would wake up and recite the following Du'a:

$$\text{اَلْحَمْدُ لله الَّذِىْ اَحْيَانَا بَعْدَ مَا اَمَاتَنَا وَاِلَيْهِ النُّشُوْرُ}$$

"All praises are for Allah! Who gives us life after death and to Him we shall return."
(al-Bukhari)

After he had made his *Wudu',* Rasulullah ﷺ would go to the *masjid* and make his *Salat* with the other believers.

After the *Salat,* the Prophet ﷺ would sit with his *Sahabah.* They would discuss things that concerned them. He would also teach them how to become better believers.

After the sun came up, Rasulullah ﷺ prayed four or eight *Raka'at*. This prayer is called *Salah al-Ishraq*. After that, he usually went home to help out with the housework.

Rasulullah ﷺ was a polite man who did not like to make surprise visits to his family or friends. He always greeted them with *"As-salamu 'alaikum"* as he entered their houses. Then he prayed for them, making the following *Du'a*:

"*As-salamu 'alaikum!*"

"O Allah! I call on You to make me enter in a good way and leave in a good way.
In the name of Allah, we enter and in the name of Allah we leave.
And in Allah, our Lord, we put our trust."
(Abu Dawud)

At home, Rasulullah ﷺ took part in the housework.

It was his Sunnah to mend his own shoes and clothes.

He used to help clean the house & make dough for bread.

He used to milk the family goat.

Sometimes he also did shopping for the family.

After making *Dhuhr Salat*, Rasulullah ﷺ would go to the market. He spent a good part of the afternoon there.

Just like a police officer on his daily patrol, Rasulullah ﷺ watched how people behaved while buying and selling. He wanted to make sure that the shop-keepers were not cheating their customers.

LESSON 19

Rasulullah ﷺ usually took a short nap after lunch and before the 'Asr Salat. This was the time of day that was the hottest. This nap is called *Qailulah* and it is a *Sunnah* to take one if we can. When it was time for 'Asr Salat, Rasulullah ﷺ would return to *Masjid* to lead the prayer.

'ASR TIME

MAGHRIB TIME

In the evening, after the *Maghrib Salat*, Rasulullah ﷺ would teach Islam to the women. They would learn about their responsibilities as *Muslimah*. Rasulullah ﷺ showed that he loved and respected everyone, male or female.

In the night, after 'Isha Salat Rasulullah ﷺ got ready for bed. He always made *Wudu'* before he went to sleep. He would put on his sleeping clothes and recite the following *Du'a* before lying down:

'ISHA TIME

اَلْحَمْدُ للهِ الَّذِيْ اَحْيَانَا بَعْدَ مَا اَمَاتَنَا وَاِلَيْهِ النُّشُوْرُ

"O Allah! In Your name I live and I die."
(al-Bukhari)

LESSON
19

TAHAJJUD TIME

Rasulullah ﷺ would also recite the Qur'an before sleeping. It was his *Sunnah* to read three short *Surahs*. He would then wake up after a few hours of sleep and pray *Salat ul-Tahajjud*

What have we learned?

- Rasulullah ﷺ led a busy life.

- All his activities were centered on *Salah*.

- Rasulullah ﷺ spent his day attending to his family's needs and the needs of the Muslim community.

- Rasulullah ﷺ was a problem-solver.

Do we know these words?

Hectic

sunrise

market

problem-solver

As you have learned, The Prophet ﷺ lived a very busy life. Look at his schedule below and then fill out yours. For example, He worked in the late morning.. are you working at school at that time? Have fun!

Think about it!

Time	Sunnah: The Prophet's Schedule	My Daily Schedule
Early Morning	Made *Wudu*, prayed *Fajr*, had breakfast & sat with *Sahabah*	
Sunrise	Prayed *Ishraq*	
Late Morning	Work: helped at home	
Noon	Prayed *Zuhr*	
Afternoon	Work: watched *ummah* in market	
Late Afternoon	Lunch, short nap	
Asr	Prayed *Asr* then stayed at *Masjid*,	
Early Evening	Prayed *Maghrib*, taught Ladies	
Evening	Dinner, prayed *Isha*	
Night	*Wudu*, Got ready for bed, Recited d'ua and Qur'an	
Late Night	Woke up, Prayed *Tahajjud*	

FAJR TIME
SUN RISE
ZUHR TIME
ASR TIME
MAGHRIB TIME
'ISHA TIME
TAHAJJUD TIME

Salawat: Our Love for Rasulullah ﷺ

Tune in!

Al-Hamdulillah!
We belong to the *Ummah* of Muhammad ﷺ.

Rasulullah ﷺ loves us. He always prays for us.
He wants us to be happy and to lead peaceful lives.
To show our gratitude for this love,
we need to feel love for Rasulullah ﷺ in our hearts.
Let us find out about making *Salawat* to our
beloved Rasulullah ﷺ and how this helps us.

Have you ever noticed that when people mention the name of Prophet Muhammad ﷺ you hear them saying the following phrase?

صلّى الله عليه وسلّم

Sal Allahu 'Alaihi wa Sallam

We call this phrase *Salawat.* Both the Qur'an and *Sunnah* require us to make *Salawat* whenever we say, hear or read the name of Rasulullah ﷺ Allah says in the Qur'an:

إِنَّ ٱللَّهَ وَمَلَـٰٓئِكَتَهُۥ يُصَلُّونَ عَلَى ٱلنَّبِىِّ

يَـٰٓأَيُّهَا ٱلَّذِينَ ءَامَنُوا۟ صَلُّوا۟ عَلَيْهِ وَسَلِّمُوا۟ تَسْلِيمًا ۝

*"Certainly Allah and His Angels send blessings on the Prophet.
O you who believe! Send blessings to him too and salute him in abundance."*
(Al-Ahzab: 56)

We show respect for Rasulullah ﷺ when we make *Salawat.* It is an act of love. It helps our hearts and minds think of Rasulullah ﷺ Allah ﷻ will reward us for making *Salawat.* The biggest reward that we can receive is Allah's blessings.

Rasulullah ﷺ once said:

"Whoever sends Salawat on me once,
Allah will send blessings on that person ten times."
(Ibn Majah)

Salawat is an easy way of thanking Rasulullah ﷺ for giving his love and kindness to us. There are many ways to make *Salawat*. Some of the phrases are long while others are short. Here are a few that we can say:

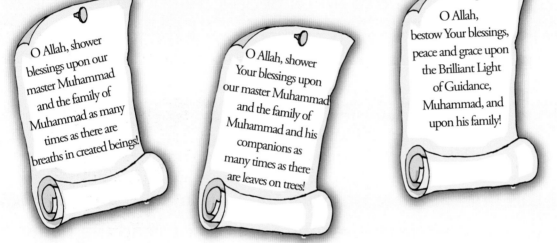

O Allah, shower blessings upon our master Muhammad and the family of Muhammad as many times as there are breaths in created beings!

O Allah, shower Your blessings upon our master Muhammad and the family of Muhammad and his companions as many times as there are leaves on trees!

O Allah, bestow Your blessings, peace and grace upon the Brilliant Light of Guidance, Muhammad, and upon his family!

Do you know that a person who does not make *Salawat* when Rasulullah's name is mentioned is considered stingy? The Prophet said:

"The stingy person is one who hears my name and does not make Salawat."
(at-Tirmidhi)

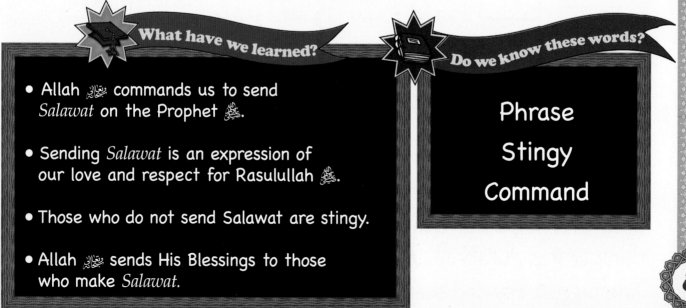

What have we learned?

- Allah ﷻ commands us to send *Salawat* on the Prophet ﷺ.

- Sending *Salawat* is an expression of our love and respect for Rasulullah ﷺ.

- Those who do not send Salawat are stingy.

- Allah ﷻ sends His Blessings to those who make *Salawat*.

Do we know these words?

Phrase

Stingy

Command

LESSON 21

The *Sahabah's* Love for Rasulullah ﷺ

The *Sahabah* were the companions of Prophet Muhammad ﷺ.
They heard his voice, saw his face and spent time with him.
The *Sahabah* loved Rasulullah ﷺ very much.
They tried their best to follow and obey him.
They loved him and always wanted to be in his company.

*"None of you becomes a real believer until
I am dearer to him than his children,
his parents and all mankind."*
(Muslim)

Let's read how four *Sahabah* showed
their undying love for Rasulullah ﷺ.

Love is a special feeling that Allah ﷻ gives to human beings. When we love someone, we care about them and we think about them all the time.

Rasulullah ﷺ said the best people after him are his *Sahabah*.
The lives of the Sahabah provide us with good examples
on how to love Rasulullah ﷺ

Abu Bakr ﷺ

The *Sahabi* who became the leader
of the *Ummah* after Rasulullah ﷺ
was Abu Bakr ﷺ.

Throughout Rasulullah's lifetime, Abu Bakr ﷺ was a close and faithful companion. He was the person who went with Rasulullah ﷺ on the *Hijrah* and hid with him in the Cave of Thawr.

When the *Kuffar* laughed at Rasulullah ﷺ when he spoke about the *Isra' and Mi'raj,* Abu Bakr ﷺ stood up and said,

> *"People of Makkah! You have never known Muhammad to be a liar!*
> *I believe whatever he says!"*

Abu Bakr was the first to believe in the *Isra' and Mi'raj.*

Umar ﷺ

One of the ways the *Sahabah* showed their love for Rasulullah ﷺ was following his example.

'Umar ﷺ once refused to accept a gift from Rasulullah ﷺ. When the Prophet ﷺ asked him why he refused the gift, 'Umar ﷺ said,

> *"O Rasulullah! Didn't you tell us that*
> *it is better not to take anything from anyone?"*

Rasulullah ﷺ was happy to find 'Umar ﷺ trying to follow the *Sunnah.* But Rasulullah ﷺ explained,

> *"Yes, 'Umar, that's true.*
> *However, when something comes to you without you asking for it,*
> *you should accept it. For it has truly been sent by Allah."*

The *Sahabah* admired Rasulullah ﷺ and they loved him deeply. He had struggled and sacrificed in order to bring Allah's last message to the world. This fact inspired the *Sahabah.* They were always ready to make sacrifices for Rasulullah ﷺ.

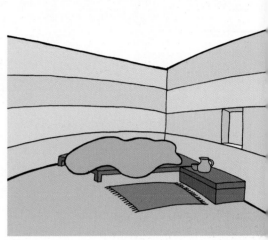

When the *Kuffar* planned to kill Prophet Muhammad ﷺ, 'Ali ؓ said he would stay in Rasulullah's house so that they would be confused. At first, Rasulullah ﷺ refused. This would put 'Ali's life in danger. However, 'Ali ؓ said,

"My beloved cousin! You are the Messenger of Allah. I love you more than my own life. Please give me the honor of giving my life for you."

Many years later, when Rasulullah ﷺ settled in Madinah, he wanted to make *Hajj*. He sent 'Uthman ؓ to talk to the *Kuffar* of Makkah. After reaching an agreement with them, 'Uthman got ready to leave. The *Kuffar* said if he wanted to he could visit the Ka'bah, but Rasulullah ﷺ could not. Instead of taking the chance to visit the Ka'bah alone, Uthman ؓ said,

"You cannot know how much we love our Prophet! How can you expect me to visit the Ka'bah when you stop the one I love from coming here?"

What have we learned?

- Love and respect for Rasulullah ﷺ are part of every Muslim's faith.

- The *Sahabah* are models for us to follow in our love for Rasulullah ﷺ.

- The *Sahabah* displayed their love for Rasul ﷺ in their commitment to follow his guidance.

- Our love for Rasulullah ﷺ requires us to make sacrifices for the cause of Islam.

Do we know these words?

Commitment

Opportunity

Sacrifice

Inspired

Think about it!

When we love someone dearly we are willing to sacrifice a lot for that person.
Think about the love of *Sahabah* ﷺ for Rasulullah ﷺ!
Now, write in the table below what the following Sahabi did because of their love for Rasulullah ﷺ.

Name	Occasion:	Actions/Reason
'Ali ﷺ	Just before Rasulullah ﷺ left his house for *Hijrah* to Madinah.	
AbuBakr ﷺ	During the *Hijrah* to Madinah in the cave of Thawr	
'Umar ﷺ	When Rasulullah ﷺ gave him a gift	
'Uthman ﷺ	When he was offered by the of Makkah to make the *Tawwaf* of the Ka'bah without Rasulullah ﷺ or another	
Khadijah ﷺ	After her marriage to Rasulullah ﷺ	
Abu Ayyub Al Ansari ﷺ	When he and his wife became the host of Rasulullah ﷺ in Madinah	

Let's Make Rasulullah ﷺ Happy

Tune in!

Rasulullah ﷺ was sent as a mercy for all.
He loved and cared for everyone he met.

There were some people that he loved very very much.
These people were those who tried
their best to make Rasulullah ﷺ happy.

Rasulullah ﷺ loved to see people with good qualities like sincerity, honesty, kindness and politeness.
It is important that we try to have these wonderful qualities.
Rasulullah ﷺ will be proud of us on the Day of Judgment if we do.

The *Sahabah* did things to make Rasulullah ﷺ happy. They could not ever think of doing something that would make him unhappy.

The day after the Prophet's daughter
Fatimah ﷺ was married, Rasulullah ﷺ
asked her why she was not wearing
a new dress he had given her as a gift. She said,

*"O Father! I gave it to a woman
who was very poor."*

Rasulullah ﷺ was not angry that she had given
away his gift. He was actually very happy to
see his daughter's care and concern for others.

One time Rasulullah ﷺ said that a lot of money
was needed to equip the Muslim army. They
needed to defend themselves from an attack.
Rasulullah ﷺ invited everyone to help out.

Many of the Sahabah saw this as an opportunity to please Allah ﷻ and to please Rasulullah ﷺ Some saw this as a chance to compete in good deeds. Who would give the most for the cause of Allah ﷻ?

Before *Maghrib Salat* both 'Umar ﷺ and Abu Bakr ﷺ came to the *masjid.* They had their donations.

'Umar ﷺ brought half of everything he owned. When Rasulullah ﷺ asked him,

"O Umar! This is a big donation! What have you left for your family?"

'Umar ﷺ replied,

"Half I brought here, O Rasulullah. The rest I left for them."

Then Rasulullah ﷺ asked Abu Bakr ﷺ,

"This is an even bigger donation. What have you left for your family Abu Bakr?"

Abu Bakr ﷺ replied,

"I left Allah and His Prophet for my family."

By having such a generous attitude, we too can make Rasulullah ﷺ happy. Although he is not here with us physically, Rasulullah ﷺ said:

"My death is a great good for you! Your deeds will be shown to me by Allah. When I see your good-ness, I shall praise Allah. When I see your sins, I shall ask Him to forgive you."
(Musnad)

LESSON 22

A Star of Guidance
Fatimah Uz-Zahra 🌸
A Sincere Muslimah

Fatimah 🌸 was the **daughter** of Muhammad ﷺ.
She was born in Makkah to Khadijah 🌸,
the beloved wife of Muhammad ﷺ.
She was born five years before the first *Wahi*.

Fatima was the last of Rasulullah's daughters after
Zainab, Ruqayya, and Umm Kulthum.

She has many
titles like:

az-Zahra
"the shining one"

and al-Batul
"the pure one"

She spent much of her time in prayer, reciting the Qur'an and
in other acts of worship.

Fatima was married to Ali 🌸.
Muslims regard Fatimah 🌸 as
a devoted daughter,
loving mother,
gifted teacher,
and sincere Muslimah.

What have we learned?

- Pleasing Rasulullah ﷺ is part of showing our love and respect towards him.

- The *Sahabah* did deeds that would make Rasulullah ﷺ happy.

- We should follow Rasulullah ﷺ so he will be proud of us on the Day of Judgment.

- The best way to please Rasulullah ﷺ is to do things that please Allah ﷻ.

Do we know these words?

Upright
Generous
Actually
Equip
Physically

Think about it!

When we love someone dearly
we are willing to sacrifice a lot for that person.
Think about the love of *Sahabah* for Rasulullah!
Now, write in the table below what the following *Sahabi* did
because of their love for Rasulullah.

Name	Occasion:	Actions/Reason
'Ali	Just before Rasulullah left his house for *Hijrah* to Madinah.	
AbuBakr	During the *Hijrah* to Madinah in the cave of Thawr	
'Umar	When Rasulullah gave him a gift	
'Uthman	When he was offered by the *Kuffar* of Makkah to make the Tawwaf of the Ka'bah without Rasulullah or another	
Khadijah	After her marriage to Rasulullah	
Abu Ayyub Al Ansari	When he and his wife became the host of Rasulullah in Madinah	

Lesson 23

The Sahabah: Role Models for Us

Tune in!

Some of the *Sahabah* received the good news that they were going to enter *Jannah*. Who were they?

What made them so special as to be promised *Jannah*?"

The *Sahabah* were very special people in the eyes of Rasulullah ﷺ He said:

> *"Do not talk bad about my companions. If you spent a mountain of gold, it would not be equal to the portion or even half of what was spent by one of them."*
> (Bukhari)

'Abdullah Ibn Mas'ud ؓ had once said,

> *"If you are willing to follow a good example, follow the steps of Muhammad's Sahabah."*

The *Sahabah* came from many different backgrounds. Most were Arabs but some of them were African, Jewish, Greek and Persian. Some of them were rich; some of them were very poor. Some of them were strong warriors while some were weak slaves, but they all loved Rasulullah ﷺ The *Sahabah* were:

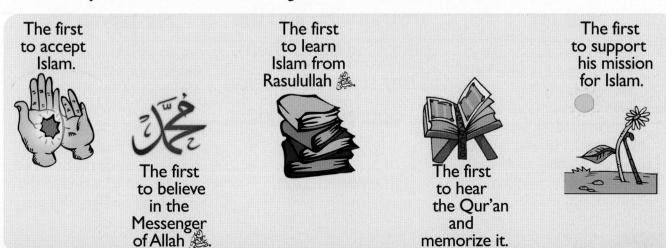

The first to accept Islam.

The first to believe in the Messenger of Allah ﷺ.

The first to learn Islam from Rasulullah ﷺ.

The first to hear the Qur'an and memorize it.

The first to support his mission for Islam.

The *Sahabah* were chosen by Allah ﷻ to accompany Rasulullah ﷺ They served him and shared the moments of happiness and sadness with him. They spent a lot of time together. They were united by Allah ﷻ to be brothers and sisters in Islam.

In the early days of Islam, the *Sahabah* joined the Prophet ﷺ to spread the message of Islam to the people of Makkah. They were his supporters during the difficult times and suffered a lot at the hands of the *Kuffar*.

Many of the companions sacrificed their lives and money for Rasulullah ﷺ Khadijah ﷺ, his wife and Abu Bakr ﷺ, his best friend, used their wealth to support his mission. They used every thing they owned to spread the message of Islam.

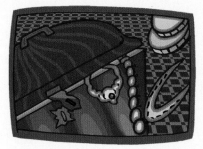

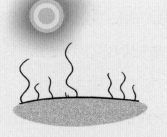

Bilal ﷺ

Bilal ﷺ was a poor slave. He suffered because he believed that Allah ﷻ was the only God and Muhammad ﷺ was His Messenger. He was forced to lie on burning sand while the *Kuffar* beat him.

The *Sahabah* believed in Rasulullah ﷺ even if it meant being laughed at by their own families and the people around them. They suffered cruelty, oppression and sometimes even death.

Sumayyah ﷺ

Sumayyah ﷺ was the first person to give her life for the sake of Islam. People who die for the cause of Allah ﷻ are called *Shahids*. A group of Kuffar stabbed Sumayyah to death because she refused to worship the old gods and goddesses.

LESSON 23

Many *Sahabah* had to suffer three years of a boycott by the leaders of the *Kuffar*. The clan of Rasulullah ﷺ and most the Muslims in Makkah were sent to live in a dry valley outside of the city. No one was allowed to trade with them or sell anything to them. The believers faced starvation. Many became sick and died, like our beloved Khadijah ؓ, the Prophet's wife.

The *Sahahbah* followed the *Sunnah* of Rasulullah,

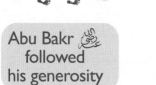

Abu Bakr ؓ followed his generosity

'Uthman ؓ followed him in his modesty.

'Umar ؓ took after Rasulullah's qualities of hard work and justice.

'Ali ؓ took after his love for knowledge and became a great scholar and a brave warrior.

We should also work hard to follow the way of Rasulullah ﷺ Although we are living in a different time, it is important to remember that the importance of being a good Muslim will never change. This is why it is important to know about the lives of Rasulullah ﷺ and his *Sahabah*.

Ibn Mas'ood ؓ said,

"Indeed Allah looked into the hearts of His servants and found the heart of Muhammad to be the best of the hearts. He chose him for Himself and sent him as a Messenger.

Then He looked into the hearts of His servants after Muhammad and found the hearts of the Sahabah to be the best of the hearts of the servants. So He made them companions of His Messenger…"

[Ahmad, at-Tayalasi]

What have we learned?

- The *Sahabah* were the first to accept Islam.

- The *Sahabah* were dedicated people who suffered hardships and oppression.

- The *Sahabah* emulated Rasulullah ﷺ in his generosity, forgiveness, and hard work.

- We learn from the examples of the *Sahabah* because their way is the way to success in this life and in the Hereafter.

Do we know these words?

Triumph

Ridiculed

Tyranny

Martyr

Necessities

Think about it!

Can you imagine how it would feel if your family was not allowed to buy food and other daily necessities from stores and then sent to a lonely place to live for three years. In the following table, write how you would find necessities and try to survive.

Item	Ways we get them now	Ways we will get them during the boycott
Food		
Water		
Clean Clothes		
Beds		
Entertainment		
Transport		

LESSON 24

Abu Bakr As Siddiq
A Noble and Gentle Friend

Rasulullah ﷺ said:

"Abu Bakr's name shall be called out from the gates of Paradise, and he will be the first of my followers to enter it."

(Sahih al-Bukhari)

"Abu Bakr"

Abu Bakr's real name was 'Abd ul-Ka'bah ibn 'Uthman. Later Rasulullah ﷺ changed his name to 'Abdullah, but everyone knew him as Abu Bakr.

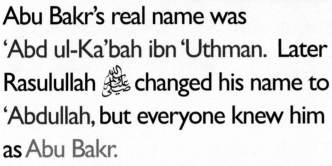

أبو بكر صديق

Fingertips

To show our respect towards the *Sahabah* we like to use the words:
"Sayyidina" (for men)
or
"Sayyidatina" (for women).
This respectful title means something like:
"our sir" or "our madam."
Some people also use the word:
"Hazrat"
which has the same meaning.

Abu Bakr ﷺ came from a noble family. His father and his mother belonged to Bani Ta'im clan. Like the Prophet's clan, the Bani Hashim, this clan was also part of the Quraish tribe.

Abu Bakr ﷺ was known for his polite and gentle character. He was honest, and truthful. He was greatly respected by people. His goodness won him the lasting friendship of the Prophet ﷺ

Keypoints

Abu Bakr ﷺ was:

The first adult male to accept Islam.

Rasulullah's faithful friend and companion.

A successful and kind-hearted business person.

Abu Bakr 🙵 had the honor of being with the Prophet ﷺ during the most dangerous days of his life. He was a faithful friend of Rasulullah ﷺ in both the good times and bad.

When Allah ﷻ commanded the Prophet ﷺ to make *Hijrah*, Abu Bakr 🙵 accompanied him during the difficult and long journey to Madinah. He sacrificed his wealth, time and health to help Rasulullah ﷺ

Abu Bakr 🙵 did not really believe in many gods and goddesses. When Rasulullah ﷺ informed Abu Bakr 🙵 that he was Allah's Messenger, Abu Bakr 🙵 believed him. He accepted Islam right away. In fact, he was the first grown man to accept Islam.

Abu Bakr 🙵 never doubted Rasulullah ﷺ He believed everything Rasulullah ﷺ said. When the Rasulullah ﷺ told the Makkans that he went on the journey of *Isra'* and *Mi'raj,* the *Kuffar* did not believe him. They said it was impossible to travel from Makkah to Jerusalem and back in one night.

However, when Abu Bakr 🙵 heard about the journey, he believed it without a doubt. Therefore, he earned the title of *as-Siddiq* – "one who supports the truth."

LESSON 24

Abu Bakr was a humble and respectable man. When the Muslims chose him to be the *Khalifah,* his first answer was that he was not the best of men for the job.

He was too humble to want to be a leader. However, the people insisted. Abu Bakr decided he would accept their offer.

He made a speech in which he said:

> "O people! I have been chosen to be your leader.
> However, I do not claim to be the best among you.
> Obey me only when I do good. If I go astray, tell me.
> Truthfulness is being honest and lying is dishonesty.
> The weakest of you will be the most important to me,
> as long as I have not helped him. In the same way,
> the strongest of you is the weakest to me as long as I have not helped the poor.
> You should keep in mind that people who stop trying to be good,
> become blameworthy in front of Allah.
> When people commit a lot of bad deeds, Allah gives them unhappiness.
> You are to follow me only as I obey Allah and His Messenger.
> If I disobey them, you will not be required to obey me."

Although Abu Bakr was Rasulullah's *Khalifah,* he did not think himself as being better than anyone.

As a leader, he continued to be a humble man. He led a very simple life. He refused to take money for his job as *Khalifah* and he continued to be a merchant. That way he could pay for his food with his own money.

This is the type of person that we should follow if Allah ever gives us leadership. May Allah bless Abu Bakr!

What have we learned?

- Abu Bakr was a close and faithful companion of Rasulullah.

- Abu Bakr earned the title As-Siddiq he who confirmed the truth because his faith was very strong.

- According to the *Sunnah* of Rasulullah, the leader of the people is responsible to serve the community and take care of its members.

Do we know these words?

Follower

Clan

Isra'

Miraj

As-Siddiq

Think about it!

Suppose you are elected to be the president of the student council. Which of the following characteristics of the Abu Bakr will you adopt and why? Give your reasons below.

Characteristic	How will you do this?	Why will you do this?
Obeying Allah		
Following the Sunnah		
Serving the Students		
Working with Shura		
Being Just and Fair		

Umar Ibn Al-Khattab ﷺ
A Reliable Leader

Tune in!

It is reported that the Messenger of Allah ﷺ said:

*"People are like mines of silver and gold;
the best of them before Islam
are the best of them when they become Muslim."*
(Sahih Muslim)

You may be wondering how is it possible for the 'best of them before Islam"
to become "the best after they come to Islam?"
Read on to find out!

'Umar ﷺ was a member of an important clan called the Bani 'Adi.
His father's name was Khattab and his mother was Hantamah.
The Bani 'Adi were part of the famous tribe of Quraish.
They were greatly respected by the people of Makkah.

When 'Umar ﷺ was a young boy,
he learned to hunt and fight.
He also learned how to be generous to guests.

'Umar ﷺ learned that
he should always follow
the traditions of his family
and tribe. He learned to
worship the gods and goddesses
of his people. He learned that
he was a nobleman, and that
poor people should serve him.

'Umar ﷺ thought it was important to defend the traditions of his people. He rarely questioned them even if they were harmful to himself or others.

When he became a man, 'Umar ﷺ was very strong. He was a loyal friend, but he had a short temper. People were careful not to make him angry, however they wanted to be his friend, because he was a powerful man.

'Umar ﷺ did not like what Rasulullah ﷺ was teaching in Makkah. He did not believe in one God. He felt that Islam made fun of his gods. It insulted the ways of his ancestors. 'Umar ﷺ refused to accept this new faith. Not only that, he decided to fight it by words and by actions.

Knowing how powerful Umar was, Rasulullah ﷺ went to the Ka'bah one night and prayed,

"O Allah! make Islam strong with either of the two men: Amr bin Hisham or 'Umar ibn al-Khattab."

Key points

'Umar ibn al-Khattab ﷺ:

• belonged to a noble family of Makkah.

• was trained in the methods of warfare.

• had a deep sense of right and wrong.

• refused to accept Rasulullah's message in the beginning.

'Umar ﷺ thought that the teachings of Rasulullah ﷺ were disturbing Makkah. He became so angry that one day he decided to kill him. He took his sword and went out to find him.

As he was going through the streets of Makkah, he met a man. The man had accepted Islam, but kept it secret because he was afraid of how the *Kuffar* would treat him. This man asked 'Umar ﷺ where he was going in such a rage with his sword drawn. 'Umar ﷺ responded,

"I am going to kill Muhammad and finish Islam!"

The man became very worried. He tried to think of a way to turn 'Umar's attention to something else. Then he could run to Rasulullah ﷺ and warn him. He said,

"'Umar! You had better look out for your own family first. Your sister and brother-in-law are Muslims. Why don't you take care of them first?"

'Umar became very upset. He decided to go to Rasulullah ﷺ later. He went directly to his sister's house. When he reached there, he heard a voice reciting something. His sister and her husband were reading the Qur'an. They heard 'Umar bang on the door and stopped and hid the Qur'an.

"Bismillah ar Rahman ar Rahim"

KNOCK! KNOCK!

When they answered the door 'Umar ﷺ was so angry at his sister that he slapped her on the face. Blood began to pour out of her mouth.

When 'Umar ﷺ saw the blood he began to feel sad. His heart began to melt. He asked his sister and her husband to show him what they were reading. They gave the Qur'an to him after he made the *Wudu'*.

'Umar ﷺ then picked up the Qur'an and read. He realized that its words could not have been written by any human. Tears came rolling down from his eyes. The miraculous power of the Qur'an changed his heart.

"O my sister," said 'Umar ﷺ with tears in his eyes, *"I have never seen or read anything so beautiful. Take me to Muhammad."*

'Umar ﷺ went straight to Rasulullah's home. He arrived at the door with his sword in his hand. He asked to see Rasulullah ﷺ

Rasulullah ﷺ asked 'Umar ﷺ to come in. 'Umar ﷺ said the *Shahadah* and accepted Islam. He became a loyal companion of Rasulullah ﷺ

Many years later 'Umar ﷺ became the *Khalifah* after Abu Bakr ﷺ. One day a poor man came to him and said,

*"O 'Umar! You are our leader.
Even if a sheep is eaten by a wolf
along the Euphrates River, you will be held responsible."*

'Umar ﷺ walked the streets of Madinah every night. He listened and checked to see if everything was all right. He made sure no one was breaking the law and that everyone had enough to eat

'Umar ﷺ was very concerned about the welfare of everyone living in the lands ruled by the Muslims. He was fair and just with all people, whether they were Muslim or non-Muslim.

One night during his rounds, 'Umar ﷺ saw a fire out in the desert. He went to investigate. There he found a woman and her children. The woman had a kettle over the fire, and her children were crying. She did not recognize 'Umar ﷺ and she thought he was just a traveler.

'Umar ﷺ asked,

"Why are these children crying?"

"Because they are hungry and I have no food to give them,"

said the woman.

"Well what is in the kettle then?"

asked 'Umar ﷺ.

"Only a bit of water. I hoped to calm them down so that they would go to sleep. Then they would forget their hunger,"

said the woman. Then she said,

"I tell you Allah will be the judge between 'Umar and me on the Day of Judgment. Look at how we are starving!"

"May Allah have mercy on you! How could 'Umar know of your troubles?"

'Umar ؓ asked .

"His is our amir, our leader. He should know all that goes on in his land,"

said the woman.

'Umar ؓ returned to Madinah and filled a bag with flour, oil, dates, clothes and also some money. Then he returned to the woman and her children.

The children and their mother were very happy. The woman thanked him and said,

"May Allah reward you for your kindness! You would make a much better amir than 'Umar!"

'Umar ؓ replied,

"Perhaps one day, when you meet the Khalifah, you will find me there." And then he left them.

What have we learned?

- 'Umar ؓ became one of the great defenders of Islam.

- A responsible leader is one who is concerned about the welfare and well-being of his or her people.

- As leaders, we need to be fair and just to all.

Do we know these words?

Slapped

Welfare

Miraculous

Loyal

Shocked

'Uthman Ibn 'Affan
A Model of Goodness

Tune in!

Rasulullah once said that
even the angels have good opinions of 'Uthman
because he was softhearted.
He was forgiving even to those who wanted to hurt him.

'Uthman observed Rasulullah's actions closely and followed his ways.
Once, he was asked why he always smiled after making his *Wudu*.
He replied that he was merely following the ways of Rasulullah.
Let's find out more about this great *Sahabi*

Sayyidina 'Uthman was born into the powerful Makkah clan of Banu Umayyah. He was born about six years after the "Year of the Elephant." His father's name was 'Affan and his mother was 'Urwa. Banu Umayyah was the most powerful clan of the Quraish.

His family members were rich business people.
When 'Uthman grew up, he became a cloth merchant.
He was among the noble young men of Makkah.
His business grew rapidly and soon
he became a successful business
person too. His wealth and position
later proved to be very helpful for
the cause of Islam.

Although he was a great businessman, 'Uthman was also a seeker of the truth. Once when he was returning from a trip to Syria, he stopped to rest. He heard a voice calling out of the desert night,

"Sleepers awake! Ahmad has come to Makkah!"

Scared by these strange words, 'Uthman could not go back to sleep. He spoke to a friend named Talha about what he heard.

Talha said he spoken to a Christian monk in Syria some time before. The monk had asked him if *"Ahmad"* had come to Makkah. When Talha asked *"who is this Ahmad?"*, the monk told him that he was going to be the last of the prophets. He said that "Ahmad" would soon tell people he was a prophet.

Keypoints

Sayyidina 'Uthman ﷺ:
• Belonged to a very noble clan of the Quraish.

• He was of a very good character.

• He was a successful businessman.

• He was among the first to accept Islam.

• He was known as a humble and modest person.

• He was given the title *"Dhu al-Nurain"* or *"possessor of two lights."*

'Uthman and Talha made the connection and hurried to Makkah. They went straight to Talha's cousin, Abu Bakr ﷺ who then took them to Rasulullah ﷺ They told the prophet about the story of the voice. Rasulullah ﷺ told them that he was indeed the Messenger of Allah. They believed him and became Muslims right there on the spot.

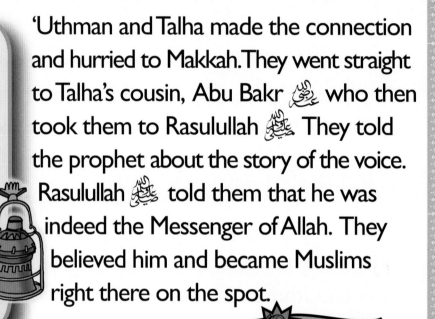

GeoLink!

Makkah

Ethiopia

Sayyidina 'Uthman married Rasulullah's daughter Ruqayyah ﷺ They loved each other very much. They made the *Hijrah* to Ethiopia with some other Muslims to escape the Kuffar. Later they left Ethiopia and moved to Madinah. Ruqayya ﷺ became very ill and passed away. 'Uthman ﷺ was very sad.

After some time had passed, Rasulullah ﷺ asked 'Uthman ﷺ if he would like to marry his third daughter, 'Umm Kulthum ﷺ Uthman accepted and after his marriage to 'Umm Kulthum ﷺ

LESSON
26

He was called *Dhu'l Nurain,* which means the one who has two lights. The daughters of Rasulullah ﷺ were those two lights.

Sayyidina 'Uthman ﷺ was also given the title of *Ghani.* It means "the generous one". He always gave generously to charitable causes and was one of the most generous persons during the lifetime of Rasulullah ﷺ

Once, the people of Madinah faced a shortage of water. The only well that could supply enough water belonged to a Jewish man. This man charged a very high price for his water and many poor people could not afford it. When Rasulullah ﷺ heard about this, he told the Muslims.

Whoever among the believers buys this well and allows everyone to use its water will be rewarded with Paradise for sure!"

'Uthman ﷺ came forward and bought the well from its owner. 'Uthman ﷺ dedicated the well for the use of all people. The People of Madinah were very grateful. You can still visit the well today when you go to Madinah.

Even before Islam, 'Uthman ﷺ led a very honest life. He was never involved in acts like gambling and drinking, which were popular with the young people at that time. When his father died and left him with a lot of money, he used the money to help the poor.

The borders of the Islamic State continued to expand during the *Khilafah* of 'Uthman ﷺ. By this time the world of Islam stretched from Morocco in the West to Afghanistan in the East. Persia, Syria, Armenia and much of the Mediterranean Sea came under Muslim rule.

After 'Umar ﷺ passed away, 'Uthman ﷺ became the *Khalifah* of the Ummah. Even after becoming a leader, he still led a simple life.

During Abu Bakr's ﷺ rule, the Qur'an was collected and put in one volume. The *Khalifah* kept this Qur'an and no other copy was made.

'Uthman ﷺ gathered a group of people who had memorized the Qur'an. He told them that people needed more copies of the Qur'an. Zaid ibn Thabit ﷺ was made the leader of the group.

THEN

The group first gathered the Qur'an into book form. It was compared to the copy that Abu Bakr ﷺ made many years before. Then they compared this written Qur'an with the recitation of those who had memorized the whole Qur'an. Because of their work and care, the Qur'an we read today is exactly as it was back then.

NOW

What have we learned?

- Sayyidina 'Uthman ﷺ belonged to a rich and powerful Makkan family of Bani Umayyah.

- He was called Dhul al-Nurain or "the man of two lights" because of his marriage to the two daughters of Rasulullah ﷺ.

- People called him *Ghani*, for being generous with his wealth.

- He was a shining example of goodness. As a leader, he was generous and humble

Do we know these words?

Successful

Nobleman

Dedicated

Recitation

Softhearted

LESSON 27

'Ali Ibn Abi Talib
The Seeker of Knowledge

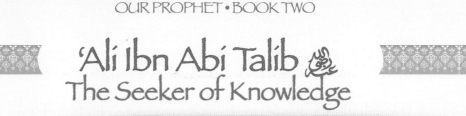

Tune in!

Among all the *Sahabah* of Rasulullah ﷺ, 'Ali ؓ was one of the most learned. Once 'Ali ؓ said:

"Praise be to Allah, there is no verse of the Qur'an that was revealed which I do not know why it was revealed, when it was revealed and to whom it was revealed."

Let's read and find out how Allah ﷻ made 'Ali ؓ one who was given knowledge and intelligence.

'Ali ؓ was the son of *Abu Talib* ؓ. Abu Talib ؓ was the brother of *'Abdullah*, who was the father of Prophet Muhammad ﷺ. This made the Prophet Muhammad ﷺ and 'Ali ؓ first cousins.

'Ali ؓ began to live with Prophet Muhammad ﷺ and Khadijah ؓ when he was a little boy. When he was nine years old, Rasulullah ﷺ received his first *Wahi*. 'Ali ؓ was the first one to believe in the message of Muhammad ﷺ and accept Islam after Khadijah ؓ.

'Ali ؓ spent his entire life from childhood until his death following the way of Rasulullah ﷺ. This had a great effect on his character.

Zainab · Hasan · Husain · Ali · Fatima · Umm Kulthuma · Ruqayya · Zainab · Abdullah · Qasim · Muhammad · Abu Talib · Abdullah · **Abdul Mutallib**

'Ali عنه married Rasulullah's beloved, and youngest daughter, *Fatimah* عنها It was a very loving and happy marriage. They had two sons, Hasan and Husain. Rasulullah ﷺ loved his grandsons very much. Both of them became great men and strong believers.

'Ali عنه was famous for his bravery and fighting skills. He defended Islam in every battle. This is how he earned the title "Asad Allah" or the "Lion of Allah."

Even though he was a brave man, 'Ali عنه was **best** known for his love of learning and knowledge. He was a great scholar and a very learned person. He was one of the few people who could read and write. 'Ali عنه wrote down the *Ayats* of the Qur'an after they were received. Eventually he had his own copy of the whole Qur'an.

'Ali عنه was an excellent writer. He was the first person to write the rules of Arabic grammar. He wrote letters on Rasulullah's behalf. He even had the honor of writing the Treaty of Hudaibiyah between the Muslims and the Quraish.

'Ali عنه spent a lot of time learning the Qur'an. He was the first person to memorize the Qur'an after Rasulullah ﷺ.

Ali ؏ lived with Rasulullah ﷺ since childhood, so he had a full knowledge of the *Sunnah*. Rasulullah ﷺ once said about 'Ali ؏,

"I am the city of knowledge and 'Ali is its gate."

After the death of 'Uthman ؏, 'Ali ؏ became the leader of the Muslims. He tried to lead with honesty, justice and compassion. Unfortunately by the time 'Ali ؏ became *Khalifah*, many troubles came to the *Ummah*.

Allah ﷻ had given the Muslims power and wealth which led them to fight among each other for these things. They forgot Rasulullah's teachings. 'Ali ؏ was killed one morning during his *Salat* by a Muslim who didn't like his decisions.

May Allah bless 'Ali ؏!

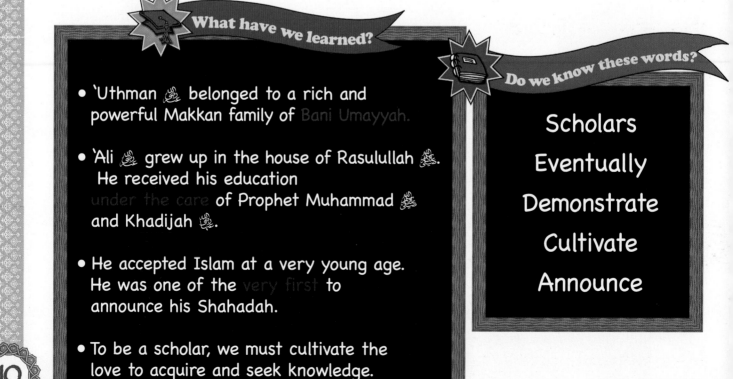

What have we learned?

- 'Uthman ؏ belonged to a rich and powerful Makkan family of Bani Umayyah.

- 'Ali ؏ grew up in the house of Rasulullah ﷺ. He received his education under the care of Prophet Muhammad ﷺ and Khadijah ؏.

- He accepted Islam at a very young age. He was one of the very first to announce his Shahadah.

- To be a scholar, we must cultivate the love to acquire and seek knowledge.

Do we know these words?

Scholars

Eventually

Demonstrate

Cultivate

Announce

Pledge of Knowledge

We just learned that 'Ali ﷺ was a great scholar and writer.
Reading, writing, and asking questions are all ways to increase our knowledge
Let us make a pledge together to increase
our learning and understanding of this world *Inshallah!*

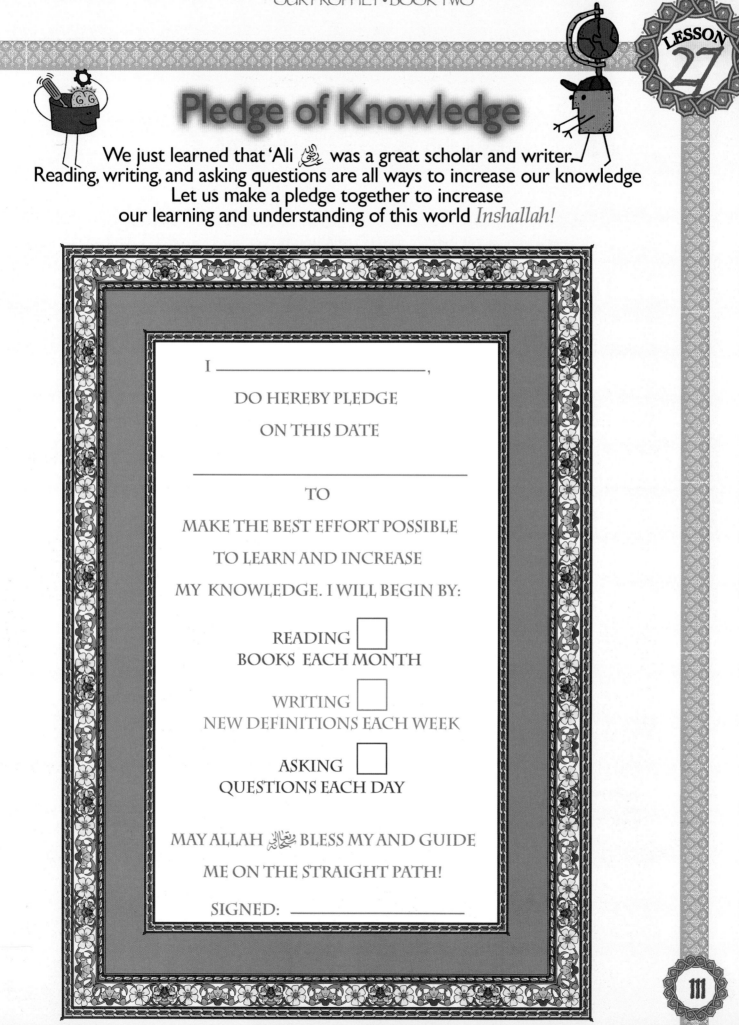

I _____,

DO HEREBY PLEDGE

ON THIS DATE

_____

TO

MAKE THE BEST EFFORT POSSIBLE

TO LEARN AND INCREASE

MY KNOWLEDGE. I WILL BEGIN BY:

READING ☐
BOOKS EACH MONTH

WRITING ☐
NEW DEFINITIONS EACH WEEK

ASKING ☐
QUESTIONS EACH DAY

MAY ALLAH ﷻ BLESS MY AND GUIDE

ME ON THE STRAIGHT PATH!

SIGNED: _____

Khadijah
The Mother of Believers

A lady so pious and noble
that her title was *Tahira,* the pure one.

She was a model for the women of her time
and a model for those to come in future generations.
Let us follow her too!

Khadijah is called *Tahirah* or "pure one" because of her honest character.

She was the daughter of Khuwailid, a successful Quraish merchant in Makkah. Khadijah grew up in a noble and educated family. When she was young, she learned a lot about business by watching her father. Because of him, she became very talented in trade.

Trading was a common way of making money in Makkah. Most people in the city made a living by buying and selling goods and supplies. Khadijah was also a business person.

Khadijah continued her family business after her father died. She single-handedly took care of it. She was a capable woman. With hard work she gained respect and recognition of other businessmen.

Makkah was a center of trade

Once Khadijah needed someone to take her goods to Syria and sell them there. She had heard of Muhammad's reputation as an honest and intelligent man. She asked him if he wanted to work for her and he agreed.

Upon Muhammad's return from Syria, Khadijah ؓ was impressed by his honesty and great business sense. He made a greater profit than expected. Muhammad ﷺ went on a few more business trips for Sayyidatina Khadijah ؓ. Those trips were also very successful.

Khadijah ؓ was so pleased with Muhammad's ﷺ honest character that she proposed marriage to him. Muhammad ﷺ agreed after consulting with his uncle, Abu Talib. They got married soon after. He was 25 years old and she was 40 years old.

Khadijah ؓ and Muhammad ﷺ shared a happy and peaceful family life together. She became his best friend.

iqra bismi rabbika......

Khadijah ؓ was very close to her husband. When the first *Wahi* came to him on Mount Hira, she was the first person to know about it. She listened to him attentively and believed him. She was the first one to accept him as a prophet of Allah. She was the very first person to embrace Islam.

Soon, their life started to change. As a wife, Khadijah ؓ supported Rasulullah ﷺ in calling people to the one God. She handled the family's affairs so that her husband could preach.

She supported the Prophet Muhammad ﷺ when nobody else would. She comforted him in difficult times. She encouraged him when the *Kuffar* of Makkah opposed him.

LESSON 28

Khadijah رضي الله عنها and Rasulullah ﷺ had six children.
Two of their sons, Qasim and Tahir (Tayib) died at a very young age.
Their four daughters, Zainab, Umm Kulthum, Ruqayyah and
Fatimah, lived to adulthood.

'Ali رضي الله عنه, Zaid رضي الله عنه and Barakah رضي الله عنها also lived in Rasulullah's house.
Khadijah رضي الله عنها took care of this big family. They lived happily together.

During the difficult years, when the *Kuffar* tried to stop Rasulullah ﷺ
from spreading Islam, Khadijah رضي الله عنها was a constant help. She tried her
best to ease the troubles.

Khadijah رضي الله عنها spent all her money for the sake
of Islam. She helped to free many believing
slaves who were treated badly by their masters.
She also used her wealth to feed the poor.

Once, the Muslims were forced to leave
their houses and stay in a hot deserted valley
on the edge of Makkah. It was a difficult time.
Khadijah رضي الله عنها became very sick. She never got
better, even when she and the other Muslims
were allowed to return to their homes.

Khadijah رضي الله عنها passed away at the age
of sixty five in the blessed month of
Ramadan. Her grave is in the *Jannat
al-Mu'alla* cemetery of Makkah.

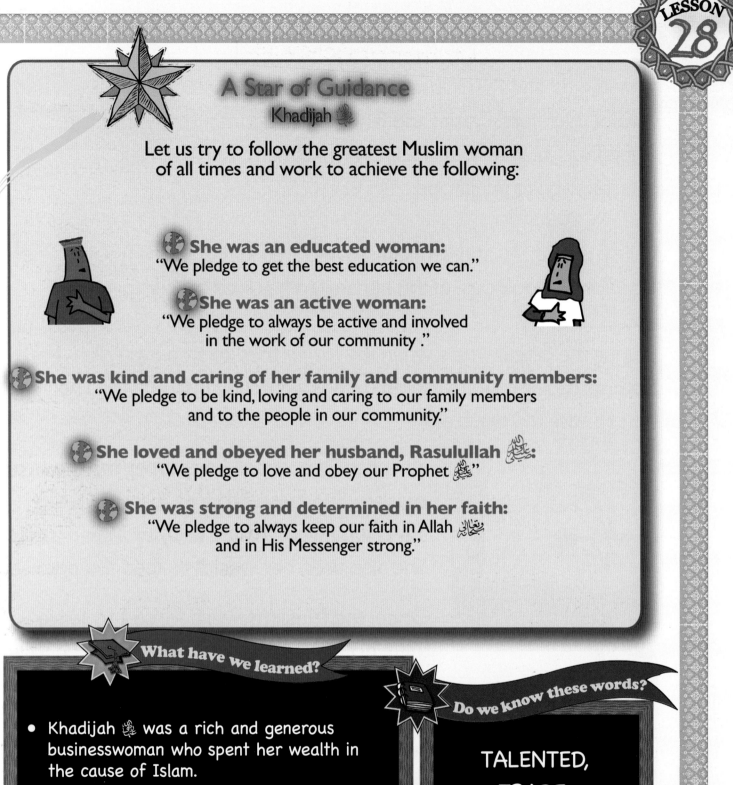

A Star of Guidance
Khadijah

Let us try to follow the greatest Muslim woman
of all times and work to achieve the following:

She was an educated woman:
"We pledge to get the best education we can."

She was an active woman:
"We pledge to always be active and involved
in the work of our community ."

She was kind and caring of her family and community members:
"We pledge to be kind, loving and caring to our family members
and to the people in our community."

She loved and obeyed her husband, Rasulullah:
"We pledge to love and obey our Prophet"

She was strong and determined in her faith:
"We pledge to always keep our faith in Allah
and in His Messenger strong."

What have we learned?

- Khadijah was a rich and generous businesswoman who spent her wealth in the cause of Islam.

- A devoted wife and a loving mother, Khadijah was respected by both the rich and poor.

- As a Muslim woman, she demonstrated commitment and made great contributions to the spread of Islam.

Do we know these words?

TALENTED,
TRADE,
REPUTATION,
SINGLE HANDEDLY,
CAPABLE,
SUPPLIES

A'ishah
The Mother of Believers

LESSON 29

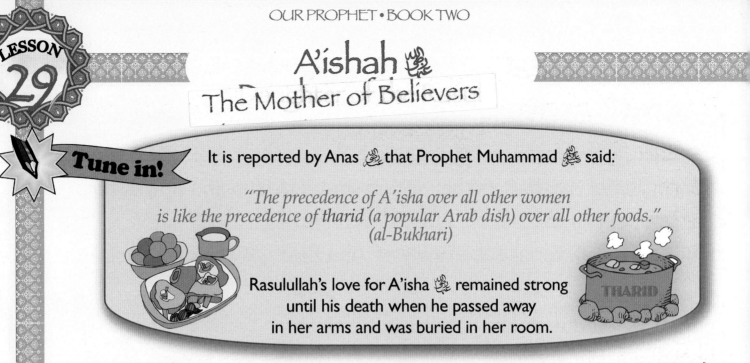

Tune in! It is reported by Anas that Prophet Muhammad said:

"The precedence of A'isha over all other women is like the precedence of tharid (a popular Arab dish) over all other foods."
(al-Bukhari)

Rasulullah's love for A'isha remained strong until his death when he passed away in her arms and was buried in her room.

THARID

A'ishah was the daughter of Abu Bakr and Umm Ruman. She was born in Makkah. Her father was a very close companion of Rasulullah. She belonged to the clan of Banu Taim, which was part of the tribe of Quraish.

A'ishah was raised as a Muslim from childhood. She said,

"I never knew my parents without them being Muslim."

Her father and mother were very close to Rasulullah, and he often visited their house. The sounds of *Adhan* and *Qur'anic recitations* were the sounds of her childhood. A'ishah and her elder sister Asma' were the first generation of Muslim children to be born in Makkah.

She was a very smart young girl. She had a very sharp memory and could remember anything she heard or saw only once. She was also a playful young girl who loved playing with dolls and running outdoors. She had many young friends and playmates in Makkah and in Madinah.

Abu Bakr ؓ migrated to Madinah with Rasulullah ﷺ before his family. A'ishah ؓ, her mother and her sisters stayed behind and prayed for their safe journey to Madinah. After a few months, Zaid ibn Harith ؓ came to Makkah to take the family of Abu Bakr ؓ back to Madinah.

A'ishah ؓ lived with her parents in Madinah. She was a bright and lively young person. She spent much of her time helping her mother and sister in the chores around the house and developing the qualities of a good Muslim.

A'ishah ؓ lived with her parents until the Battle of Badr. After the victory, she was married to the Prophet ﷺ. She then moved into his house as his wife.

Rasulullah ﷺ had a room built for A'ishah ؓ next to the *Masjid al-Nabawi.* It became known as the "room of revelation" because Rasulullah ﷺ received many revelations when he was in this room.

A'ishah ؓ spent her time learning from Rasulullah ﷺ and following his *Sunnah.* A'ishah ؓ received a great deal of attention from the community because of Rasulullah's love for her. She had a great concern for the community, especially for its women.

Many things happened when they were together that affected all the Muslims. One time, A'ishah ﷺ was traveling with Rasulullah ﷺ and a group of believers in the desert when she lost a necklace borrowed from her sister. They both spent hours looking for it. The time for *Salat al-Fajr* was almost ending and they were at a place where there was no water to make *Wudu'*.

People began to complain that A'ishah ﷺ was to blame for making the group miss the Salah. At that moment, Allah ﷻ sent revelation to Prophet Muhammad ﷺ that described how to make *Tayammum* if there was no water available.

A'ishah ﷺ had a very sharp and retentive memory. It was because of her keen intelligence and memory, that she could remember Rasulullah's sayings and revelations accurately.

She is one of the leading narrators of the *Hadith.* Women often came to A'ishah ﷺ with questions and problems.

She would give them advice according to the *Qur'an* and the *Sunnah.* If she did not know the answers she would ask for Rasulullah's help and find solutions. A'ishah ﷺ became a wise counselor and educator of the Muslims in Madinah.

A'ishah ﷺ grew up under the loving care and guidance of Rasulullah ﷺ.
She lived with him until he passed away.
She was with him when he passed away.
Rasulullah ﷺ actually died and was buried in A'ishah's room.

Once A'ishah had a dream in which three moons appeared in her room. When she told this dream to her father, he told her that if her dream were true it meant that three of good people would be buried in her room. When Rasulullah was buried in her room, Abu Bakr told her,

"That is the best of your moons."

In the years after that, both Abu Bakr and 'Umar were also buried there next to Rasulullah.

A'ishah lived for almost 50 years after Rasulullah. She became the most respected and trusted teacher of *Hadith*. She continued to teach what she learned from her blessed husband. People came to visit her and seek her advice from far and near.

What have we learned?

- A'ishah was the youngest daughter of Abu Bakr.

- She was married to Rasulullah.

- In her ten years with Rasulullah, she learned a lot from him.

- She became one of the greatest narrators of Hadiths.

- A'ishah had great interest for the education of Muslims, especially women.

- Rasulullah died in her room and he was buried there.

Do we know these words?

Talented
Playmates
Revelations
Complain
Narrator
Counselor

Learning the Sirah of Rasulullah ﷺ

Tune in!

*O Prophet! Truly we have sent you as a witness,
a bearer of glad tidings and a warner,
and as one who invites to Allah's (grace) by
His permission and as a lamp spreading light."*
(Al-Ahzab: 45:46)

The Qur'an declares Prophet Muhammad ﷺ
as the best model for all mankind.
His life is full of inspiration and guidance for everyone.
What was his lifestyle like?
What methods did he use to turn the worst people into the best citizens?
How can we learn about his noble life?

Reading and learning about the life of our
noble Prophet ﷺ is necessary for all believers.
The life story of Rasulullah ﷺ is called the *Sirah*.
We read his *Sirah* because Prophet Muhammad ﷺ
is Allah's Messenger and his deeds are examples
for all of us. Allah ﷻ says in the Qur'an:

Key points

Sirah is the writing on the life of Prophet Muhammad ﷺ.

Muslim must read and learn the *Sirah* of Rasulullah ﷺ

هُوَ ٱلَّذِى بَعَثَ فِى ٱلْأُمِّيِّـۧنَ رَسُولًا مِّنْهُمْ يَتْلُواْ عَلَيْهِمْ
ءَايَـٰتِهِۦ وَيُزَكِّيهِمْ وَيُعَلِّمُهُمُ ٱلْكِتَـٰبَ وَٱلْحِكْمَةَ وَإِن
كَانُواْ مِن قَبْلُ لَفِى ضَلَـٰلٍ مُّبِينٍ ٢

*"It is He who has sent amongst the unlettered, a Messenger of their own,
to recite to them His signs, to purify them, and to instruct them in Scripture
and Wisdom, although they had been before in manifest error."*
(Surah Al-Jumu'ah: 2)

Allah ﷻ sent Prophet Muhammad ﷺ to be a blessing for all of us.
Rasulullah ﷺ taught us *Tawhid,* belief in one God.
He also gave us the *Qur'an,* the final message from Allah ﷻ.

Rasulullah ﷺ showed us how to worship Allah ﷻ and have *Taqwah.*
He also showed us the ways to live with our family members, our friends, neighbors and other people in this world.

When we study the life Rasulullah ﷺ and follow his example, Allah ﷻ will be happy with us. As we study his life, we try to acquire the characteristics which are liked by him and Allah ﷻ.
We also begin to try to give up thoughts or actions that are *Haram* and disliked by Allah ﷻ and His Prophet ﷺ

The *Sirah* has stories about events that happened in the life of Rasulullah ﷺ
It tells the story of his life, from his child-hood in Makkah to his passing away in Madinah.

MADINAH

MAKKAH

SAUDI ARABIA

Reading the *Sirah* is not like reading other stories or legends.
We need to understand that Muhammad ﷺ is a prophet and a messenger from Allah. The stories of his life can give us success in this life and the next. There are many examples that show us how to live our lives.

SUCCESS

In the *Sirah*, we can read about Rasulullah's hard work and honesty.
We can read about his kindness and generosity.
We can read about his patience and trust in
Allah ﷻ when he faced problems and difficulties.
We can do the same.

We study hard in school.

We are honest to everyone

We are kind to both our friends. We participate in all activities that help people

HA! HA!

and avoid getting involved in activities which hurt or harm.

Studying and thinking about the life of Rasulullah ﷺ helps us to take on his characteristics. We can be kind, fair, truthful, polite, smart, helpful, and caring just like him. This is how we learn from and appreciate the *Sirah* of our dear Prophet ﷺ.

Muslim scholars have made great efforts to collect the *Hadiths* of Rasulullah ﷺ. As we know, *Hadiths* tell us about the actions and practices of Rasulullah ﷺ. *Hadiths* are important sources for the *Sirah*.

There are many biographies written about Rasulullah ﷺ.
We can read the *Sirah* in many languages.
Go to your nearest Islamic bookstore and see
if you can find an interesting *Sirah* book.

We should keep on reading more books about Rasulullah ﷺ.
We can also study the *Sirah* with our teachers.
We can listen to scholars who have special knowledge of the *Sirah*.

In the Footsteps of Rasulullah

It is important for all of us to study, learn and follow the *Sunnah* and *Hadiths* of our dear Rasulullah ﷺ

As we read these books and try to follow whatever we have learned about Rasulullah ﷺ, we have taken the first step towards becoming closer to our beloved Prophet, Muhammad ﷺ.

What have we learned?

- The Sirah talks about the life of Rasulullah ﷺ.

- The Sirah gives us knowledge of how to be just, honest, knowledgeable and much more.

- We study the Sirah so that we can learn about Rasulullah ﷺ.

- The Qur'an and Hadiths can be sources of the Sirah ﷺ.

Do we know these words?

Biography
Taqwa
Haram